SPORTS
NUTRITION

NOTE
This publication was written by registered dietitians to provide insights into better eating habits to promote health and wellness. It does not provide a cure for any specific ailment or condition and is not a substitute for the advice and/or treatment given by a licensed physician.

First published in French in 2015 by Les Publications Modus Vivendi Inc. under the title *Nutrition sportive*.
© Stéphanie Côté, Philippe Grand and Les Publications Modus Vivendi Inc., 2016

MODUS VIVENDI PUBLISHING
55 Jean-Talon Street West
Montreal, Quebec H2R 2W8
CANADA

modusvivendipublishing.com

Publisher: Marc G. Alain
Editorial director: Isabelle Jodoin
Editorial assistant and copy editor: Nolwenn Gouezel
English-language editor: Carol Sherman
Translators: Brandie Brunner and Kristin Cairns
Proofreader: Maeve Haldane
Graphic designers: Émilie Houle and Gabrielle Lecomte
Food photographer: André Noël (anoelphoto.com)
Food stylist: Gabrielle Dalessandro
Authors' photographer: David Moore (artistikdaimo.com)
Additional photography:
Pages 5, 9, 11, 29, 30, 39, 45, 47, 48, 53, 59, 76 to 84, 86, 89, 90 to 92,
95, 110 and 190: Dreamstime.com
Pages 6, 13, 15, 16, 19, 23, 25, 32, 35, 40, 51, 55, 57, 63, 70, 114, 118, 124, 127,
134, 138, 148, 160, 188, 194, 197 and 198: iStock

ISBN: 978-1-77286-000-9 (PAPERBACK)

ISBN: 978-1-77286-001-6 (PDF)
ISBN: 978-1-77286-002-3 (EPUB)
ISBN: 978-1-77286-003-0 (KINDLE)

Legal deposit — Bibliothèque et Archives nationales du Québec, 2016
Legal deposit — Library and Archives Canada, 2016

We gratefully acknowledge the financial support of the Government of Canada through the Canada Book
Fund (CBF) for our publishing activities.

Government of Quebec – Tax Credit for Book Publishing – Program administered by SODEC

Printed in Canada

SPORTS NUTRITION

21 DAYS OF MENUS

Stéphanie Côté and Philippe Grand, RD

MODUS VIVENDI

CONTENTS

INTRODUCTION

Regardless of your athletic goals and motives, whether you spin for an hour three times a week or are training for an ultramarathon, your diet affects not just your performance, but the enjoyment you get from working out.

The nutritional needs of athletes vary tremendously from one sport to another. This book focuses on endurance sports, such as running, hiking, cycling, cross-country skiing, snow-shoeing, swimming and so on. However, you will also find it useful if you enjoy activities such as tennis, Zumba or any other cardio workout, including outdoor boot camp, cardio boxing and stroller cardio.

The first part of this book teaches you where and how your body gets the energy it needs and provides key information about sports nutrition, including both general and specific recommendations (for before, during and after exercise). The second part provides 21 days of menus based on your training and competition schedule so you will have energy at the right times and can recover more easily on rest days. Finally, the third part contains nearly 50 recipes designed to meet the needs of athletes who like to eat healthy, tasty foods, but also want to spend more time in their running shoes than in the kitchen!

SPORTS NUTRITION

"You are a machine!" Maybe someone has said this to you, or perhaps you have made the same comment to an athlete who seems to have "superhuman" ability. This is also a perfect metaphor for understanding the ins and outs of sports nutrition.

Your body is your machine. You can demand a lot from it, providing you take good care of it. You have to give it the right fuel, in the right amounts, at the right times, and you have to supply it with raw materials to repair any damaged parts. Plus, every day, you must give it the input it needs to maintain, or even improve, your engine performance. That is where diet comes in: it is important for all these reasons and more. Developing and maintaining good muscle mass (which is essential to improving speed, endurance, technique and performance) also depends in large part on food, which also influences heart and lung capacity.

Sports nutrition consists in determining what and how much to eat before, and perhaps during, physical effort in order to create and conserve energy. But it is also about what to eat between and after training sessions and competitions to recover properly. For athletes, eating wisely enables you to tackle your training sessions with energy, face competitions and meet challenges with confidence, push yourself and go beyond your limits. Plus it ensures you have energy every day and enjoy training even more.

A BRIEF LESSON IN BIOLOGY

ENERGY EXPENDITURE

We need energy to breathe and digest, to make our hearts beat and maintain our body temperature, to make our brain function — in sum, we need it to stay alive. This mandatory energy expenditure is called the **basal metabolic rate.**

As with all other forms of energy expenditure, the basal metabolic rate is measured in calories (or joules in the International System of Units). It is mainly based on your age, gender and body. Metabolism usually slows as we age. It is higher in men than in women because men have more muscle mass and for various other reasons. The basal metabolic rate is estimated at approximately 1200 calories per day for women and 1600 calories per day for men. Many athletes and sports enthusiasts have a higher basal metabolic rate, about 1500 and 1800 calories per day for women and men respectively. These figures are provided simply to give a sense of magnitude. Determining an accurate basal metabolic rate takes highly sophisticated equipment that measures and analyzes the air you breathe. For practical purposes, we tend to use mathematical formulas, but they only provide an estimate of your true basal metabolic rate. These formulas take into account age, gender, height and weight. They are never completely accurate.

To estimate the energy spent over the course of a day, you have to add to this basal metabolic rate the **energy expended during routine activities,** such as showering, walking, talking and so on. These activities require about 600 extra calories per day.

Adding the basal metabolic rate and energy spent on routine activities, we see that the approximate daily caloric intake is around 2100 for female athletes and 2400 calories for male athletes. That is the energy expended without exercising. But, because we are enthusiastic athletes, we spend a little or a lot more energy than that.

To estimate your total energy expenditure, now you have to add the **energy expended during sports** to the first figures. How do you calculate this? And, more importantly, does it matter? It all depends on your goal.

WHY CALCULATE THE ENERGY YOU EXPEND WHEN EXERCISING?

It is important to have a somewhat accurate sense of the amount of energy spent and, above all, not to overestimate it when, for example, you want to lose weight. It is dangerous to believe that because you are expending a lot of energy, you are justified in eating larger servings or stopping at the ice cream shop because you think you have "room to spare" or "earned some credit." You should know that you burn fewer calories in an hour of cycling or running than you ingest when you eat an Oreo Blizzard or an Extra Value Meal at McDonald's!

Calculating how much energy you expend during sports can also be useful when you are trying to build muscle mass or when you are losing or gaining weight but do not know why. In sum, it is helpful whenever you have an issue with weight or a lack of energy.

If you are happy with your weight, have sufficient energy to exercise and eat enough to satisfy your hunger, you may wish to question the relevance of this estimate. Remember that, in order for our energy expenditure calculations to serve any purpose, we must also calculate our calorie intake, which means weighing and measuring everything we eat. This makes it hard to enjoy eating.

HOW DO YOU CALCULATE THE ENERGY EXPENDED DURING SPORTS?

You can estimate it using charts or even an ultra-sophisticated wristwatch. However, you must remember that these are only estimates and the margins of error are rather large. Nevertheless, here are some numbers to give you a general idea.

ACTIVITY (ONE HOUR)	ENERGY SPENT (in calories)	
	ATHLETE WEIGHT 120 lbs (55 kg)	ATHLETE WEIGHT 176 lbs (80 kg)
Hiking	330	480
Biking	440	640
Swimming	440	640
Cross-country skiing	490	720
Running	550	800

ESTIMATED TOTAL ENERGY EXPENDITURE

Total daily energy expenditure
= Basal metabolic rate
+ Energy expended during routine activities
+ Energy expended during sports

As an example, consider runners who train for one hour each day.
WOMAN: 1500 + 600 + 550 = **2650 calories**
MAN: 1800 + 600 + 800 = **3200 calories**

WATER LOSS
WHERE DOES YOUR FLUID INTAKE GO?

Water is notably found in the blood, where it helps carry nutrients and oxygen. It moves through the kidneys, which work as filters. Water is found in saliva and hydrates our mucous membranes. Plus it enables the body to maintain its temperature through perspiration and much more. This water constantly needs to be replenished because your body eliminates it through urine, stools, sweat and the air you exhale. You must compensate for this loss by drinking and eating.

HOW MUCH SHOULD YOU DRINK EACH DAY?

You need approximately 10 cups (2.5 liters) of fluid per day, plus more depending on your exercise regimen. Through perspiration alone, an athlete can lose anywhere from 1½ cups (375 ml) to 8 to 12 cups (2 to 3 liters) of water per hour, depending on his or her body, the type of activity and weather conditions. You do not just sweat when you are exercising outdoors on a scorching day. You also perspire when temperatures are cool and even when you are in the water.

Foods supply an average of 4 cups (1 liter) of water per day. This means you have to drink at least 4 to 6 cups (1 to 1.5 liters) of fluids per day — plus more when you exercise.

KEY NUTRIENTS AND WATER

Food provides carbohydrates, fats, proteins, vitamins and minerals, each of which play different roles. Some supply energy, while others help use up this energy, contribute to building and maintaining bones and muscles or stimulate our immune system. There are also nutrients that help you stay focused when you need it.

Eating a varied diet enables you to get all the nutritional elements you need. No single food can achieve this. Nutrition is a team sport. Moreover, it is pleasurable to eat a variety of foods and avoid monotony.

WHERE DOES ENERGY COME FROM?

The energy we need comes from food: mostly carbohydrates (sugars) and fats (lipids) and, to a lesser extent, proteins. Vitamins, minerals and water do not supply calories (and thus do not supply energy), but they are no less essential to proper body function.

Carbohydrates are the body's preferred fuel because these are the nutrients the body absorbs the fastest. During digestion, they are converted to glucose, which goes straight into the blood to deliver energy to cells. Carbohydrates that are not used immediately are stored in the form of glycogen in the liver and muscles. The glycogen reserves in the liver are used between meals to give cells the energy they need; they are depleted in a few hours when the body is at rest, but much faster during physical effort. As for the glycogen reserves in the muscles, the muscles use them when they are working.

Fats are not absorbed directly in the same way as glucose. They must pass through the liver before being converted to a usable energy source, so the body draws energy from its fat reserves. Some fat is stored in the muscles, but most of it is stored in the adipocytes (fat cells) that are scattered everywhere under our skin and around our organs. In extremely fit athletes, muscles burn the fat that is stored in them more easily than in less fit athletes and non-athletes. As for the fat stored in adipose tissue, it must go through a series of stages before it becomes energy that cells can access; this process takes longer than with glycogen.

Aside from the speed of use, the biggest difference between carbohydrates and fats is the quantity stored in the body. Glycogen reserves, although they may be bursting at the seams before a workout, are depleted in fewer than two hours of intense exercise. It is beneficial for all athletes to have good reserves regardless of their sport, but especially for endurance sports, long training sessions and tournaments where there is little downtime between events.

Meanwhile, fat reserves contain several thousand calories – even in people who are thin. However, you cannot rely solely on these reserves to feel driven or even sustained because the body does not process fats as quickly or efficiently as carbohydrates – except in the case of some endurance and ultra-endurance athletes who, over time, manage to train their bodies to dip into their fat reserves far more quickly than most athletes.

In any event, do not rely on your glycogen and fat reserves alone to get you through a long workout. You should always remember to refuel along the way if you want to finish your race. This rule applies to all sports.

What about **protein**? Protein does not deliver much energy when you are in good health and eat a proper diet: it provides no more than 5% of your fuel. The essential role of protein is building (see "Proteins," p. 24).

HOW DOES THE BODY USE ENERGY?

No matter what, whether you are resting or exercising (strength or endurance training), your energy comes from carbohydrates and fats in varying amounts.

They are used in equal measure for exercises perceived as somewhat hard, meaning activity at an intensity level of 70% of your VO2 max, or maximal oxygen consumption (see chart on opposite page). At higher intensity levels, more energy comes from carbohydrates than from fats because the energy has to be available quickly. When you exert yourself at a very high level of intensity, such as during sprinting intervals, you are burning carbohydrates almost exclusively. On the other hand, during extended or low intensity exercise, fats are contributing more because the body has time to convert and use them.

The Borg Rating of Percived Exertion Scale (RPE) is a subjective way to assess effort and give it a sense of scope. The lowest level on the scale (0) corresponds to a lack of physical effort and the highest level (10 here, but there are versions of the scale that range up to 20) equals the hardest level of exertion you can produce. Coaches can use the Borg Scale, for example, to convey to their athletes the level of intensity expected from them.

BORG SCALE		PERCEIVED INTENSITY OF EFFORT	RELATIVE INTENSITY (as %)
0	☺	NO EXERTION AT ALL	20
0.5	☺	EXTREMELY EASY	30
1	☺	VERY EASY	40
2	☺	EASY	50
3	☺	MODERATELY EASY	60
4	☺	SOMEWHAT DIFFICULT	70
5	☹	DIFFICULT	80
6	☹	MODERATELY DIFFICULT	85
7	☹	VERY DIFFICULT	90
8	☹	VERY, VERY DIFFICULT	95
9	☹	EXTREMELY DIFFICULT	100
10	☹	EXHAUSTING	110

KEY NUTRIENTS

Whether you are resting or exercising, all nutrients have complementary roles to play in the body: supplying energy, building bones and muscles, helping to carry messages between the brain and your different body parts, and so on. The nutrients you need the most are carbohydrates, fats, proteins and water. Vitamins and minerals are very important, of course, but are required in smaller quantities.

CARBOHYDRATES

Carbohydrates, also known as sugars, are divided into three broad categories: simple carbohydrates, complex carbohydrates and dietary fiber. Carbohydrates account for more than half the calories in your diet. They provide four calories per gram (except for fiber, which is not a source of energy because the body cannot digest it).

- **Simple carbohydrates** (e.g. glucose, fructose) are commonly found in table sugar, brown sugar, maple syrup, fruits, vegetables, milk and candy, as well as in gels, chews, beverages and other products for athletes.

- **Complex carbohydrates** (e.g. starch, maltodextrin) are found in bread, pasta, rice, breakfast cereals, potatoes, legumes and some specialty products for athletes.

- Unlike other carbohydrates, **dietary fiber** does not provide energy, but it still has several benefits. In particular, it makes meals more filling and promotes bowel regularity. It is found in whole-grain breads and cereals, legumes, nuts, seeds, fruits and vegetables.

The efficiency of carbohydrates in providing energy

For a long time, complex carbohydrates were described as "slow sugars" and simple carbohydrates were considered "fast sugars," but it is actually more complicated than that. How effective carbohydrates are at supplying energy quickly does not just depend on their structure (simple versus complex carbohydrates). Their **glycemic index** is also a determining factor. This refers to the speed with which carbohydrates are absorbed and released into the blood stream and, therefore, made available to muscles. For example, although glucose and fructose are both simple carbohydrates, glucose is absorbed faster than fructose. We say that it has a higher glycemic index. Meanwhile, maltodextrins are absorbed very fast although they are chains of multiple glucose molecules.

The glycemic index concept is rather complex because it is rare to find just one type of sugar in any given food. Furthermore, a food's glycemic index varies according to several factors: degree of ripeness (for fruits and vegetables), size, cooking method, degree of doneness, etc. In addition, be aware that the glycemic index of a given food does not mean anything in the context of a meal because other foods influence how quickly it will be digested.

So what is the point of knowing the glycemic index of foods? It is useful when you are choosing what to eat before, during or after exercise: when your energy, performance and recovery depend on how fast you give energy to your body.

But there's no need to fret: the nutritional recommendations provided in this book (see "Recommendations before, during and after exercise," p. 49) take glycemic index values into account. Note that anyone who is following the principles of healthy eating is primarily consuming foods with a low or moderate glycemic index (e.g. fruits, vegetables, whole-grain products, legumes, fish, nuts and other staples). Quite often, foods with a high glycemic index (e.g. refined grain products, pastries, sugary beverages) have less nutritional value.

DAILY CARBOHYDRATE NEEDS ACCORDING TO ATHLETE TYPE AND PHYSICAL ACTIVITY
(approximate figures for an adult)

No physical activity	Approximately 4 g per kg of body weight
Slim athletes in aesthetic sports (diving, gymnastics)	4 to 5 g per kg of body weight
Most athletes	Approximately 6 g per kg of body weight
Athletes who train at high intensity levels for more than 3 hours per day	7 to 10 g per kg of body weight

Carbohydrate content of foods

FOOD	CARBOHYDRATE CONTENT (in g)
1 cup (250 mL) cooked lentils	40
1 slice whole wheat bread, 1 ½ oz (45 g)	40
½ cup (125 ml) cooked macaroni	23
1 small apple	15
½ cup (125 ml) orange juice	15
1 cup (250 ml) milk	13
1 tbsp maple syrup	13
1 cup (250 ml) soy milk	8
1 cup (250 ml) almond milk	8
½ cup (125 ml) carrots	7
½ cup (125 ml) sliced strawberries	7
½ cup (125 ml) plain Greek yogurt	6
½ cup (125 ml) plain regular yogurt	5

FATS

Fats, or lipids, perform several functions. In particular, they are a component of every cell in your body, especially the cells in your nervous system. They make it possible to absorb certain vitamins and to produce hormones. They also provide energy: nine calories per gram.

There are several types of fats and each has its own advantages and drawbacks. Their impact on your body and your health depends on how much you consume. Beyond the type of fat, you should also pay attention to the type of food it comes from. A fatty food that also provides an array of nutritional elements is far worthier than a fatty food that has no nutritional value. Cheese, for example, is a far more suitable choice than a corn dog or french fries, just as nuts are better than a croissant. Eating healthfully does not mean banning certain foods based on a particular nutritional argument. Rather, it is about paying attention to the quantity, frequency, quality and variety of your diet.

Meat, poultry, fatty fishes (salmon, herring, sardines, etc.), nuts, seeds, peanuts, avocados, olives, tofu, yogurt, cheese and eggs are sources of fat that provide an abundance of nutrients and have a rightful place in your everyday menus. However, charcuterie, french fries, breaded and fried foods, Danishes and pastries, for example, should be included in your diet far less often and only in small servings.

PROTEIN

Protein is needed to build muscles, hair, skin and nails. Protein is essential for repairing and replacing these when necessary, such as your skin after a wound, your muscles after an intense workout or your nails after a very long run. Protein also contributes to the proper functioning of the immune system, hormone system and chemical reactions in your body.

Although protein is critical to your cells, it supplies very little energy if you are in good health and eating a proper diet. Theoretically, it provides four calories per gram. "Theoretically" because in reality, protein is only used for fuel in situations where you are eating very little because of a weight-loss diet or illness. During exercise, the energy contribution from protein is negligible. Indeed, the process of converting it for use by the muscles you are working is very labor intensive.

Although protein is used to maintain and increase muscle mass, it does not do the job on its own. Protein intake must be combined with training to achieve significant results. Protein is stored in your muscles. It is impossible to build protein reserves beyond the muscles' storage capacity, which is why you have to eat foods that contain proteins at each meal. That being said, there is no point in eating tons of protein because the body is unable to process it beyond a certain amount. The surplus is excreted or converted into fat like all other calories that exceed the body's needs.

For example, an endurance athlete who weighs 176 lbs (80 kg) must eat at least 96 g (0.55 x 176) of proteins each day, but will not derive any benefit from eating more than 128 g (0.73 x 176). (See the daily protein needs table based on physical activity, p. 25.)

DAILY PROTEIN NEEDS ACCORDING TO PHYSICAL ACTIVITY (approximate figures for an adult)	
No physical activity	0.8 to 1.2 g per kg of body weight
Endurance sports (running, cycling, swimming, etc.)	1.2 to 1.6 g per kg of body weight
Strength sports (weight lifting, sprinting, etc.)	1.6 to 1.8 g per kg of body weight
Aesthetic sports (dancing, gymnastics, etc.)	1.2 to 1.7 g per kg of body weight

The total amount of protein should be spread over your meals and snacks because the body can effectively use about 1 oz (30 g) at a time. This means there is no point in eating 2 lbs (1 kg) of steak in the evening if you neglected proteins throughout the day. You should aim for ½ to 1 oz (15 to 30 g) of protein at each meal, depending on your needs. Not only does this amount of protein make muscle protein production more effective, it also makes your meals more filling. By including one or several good protein sources in each meal and snack, it is absolutely possible to eat the necessary quantities. Supplements are not generally needed.

Protein content of foods

FOOD	PROTEIN CONTENT (in g)
½ chicken breast (3 ½ oz/100 g)	33
1 small patty of lean ground beef (3 ½ oz/100 g)	28
3 ½ oz (100 g) sardines	21
5 oz (150 g) extra-firm tofu	21
1 cup (250 ml) cooked lentils	18
¾ cup (175 ml) Greek yogurt	16
1½ oz (50 g), or 1-inch (2.5 cm) cube Cheddar cheese	12
¾ cup (180 ml) regular yogurt	10
1 cup (250 ml) milk	9
½ cup (125 ml) roasted almonds	8
2 tbsp peanut butter	7
1 cup (250 ml) soy milk	6
1 large egg	6
1 cup (250 ml) almond milk	1

VITAMINS AND MINERALS

We could draw up a long list of all the vitamins and minerals and explain why they are important for athletes: calcium, potassium, magnesium and others, for muscle and cardiac contractions and transferring nerve inputs between the brain and the rest of the body; iron to carry oxygen in the blood; vitamin B12 to produce red blood cells and so on. But the most important thing to remember is that if you have a varied diet and eat enough foods to cover your energy needs (if your weight remains constant, that is a good sign), it is highly likely that you are getting all the vitamins and minerals you need.

That said, some situations put you at a higher risk of deficiencies:

- If you are following a weight-loss diet (e.g. fewer than 1200 calories per day)

- If you are excluding several foods from your diet (e.g. vegetarianism, gluten free)

- If you are a female runner. Women have a higher risk of iron deficiency, especially because of their monthly blood loss. This risk is more pronounced in women who run because the impact of running causes red blood cells to burst in the soles of the feet.

WATER

Water is everywhere in the body: in fact, it accounts for two-thirds of your total body mass and three-fourths of muscle mass. Blood also contains a lot of water. Since blood is what carries oxygen and other nutrients (including sugar) to your muscles, proper hydration is crucial to sustaining physical activity.

Water also plays a role in cooling down the body. During workouts, muscles generate a lot of heat that must be discharged to prevent dangerous rises in body temperature. This heat is dissipated when liquid is released in the form of perspiration.

Inadequate hydration affects performance and concentration. This means that good hydration is essential for optimal athletic performance. While drinking water is the best way to stay hydrated, it is not the only way. You can also have juices, milk, sports beverages, tea, coffee and herbal infusions, along with soups, stews, smoothies etc. Even solid foods provide water. For example, the water content of fruits and vegetables ranges from 85 to 95%.

To know your water needs, see the recommendations on p. 36.

GENERAL FOOD
Recommendations

Diet is a critical factor for athletes, as are physical training, sleep and mental preparation. Neglecting any of these areas will have harmful consequences. Your muscle development may not be optimal if your diet is not optimal. You may run out of energy or lack concentration, or even become disoriented. Plus, you will not recover as well after a training session. In short, if you have a poor diet, you will never go as fast, as high or as far as you could if you ate well.

But be careful not to think about food solely in terms of performance, because that could bring on unnecessary stress. Eating well should not become an obsession.

RECOMMENDATIONS:

1. Eat balanced meals
2. Eat filling foods
3. Drink enough water
4. Have snacks as needed
5. Drink alcohol in moderation
6. Limit consumption of processed foods
7. Watch out for deficiencies if you are vegetarian
8. Do not opt for a gluten-free diet without a medical reason
9. Be disciplined, but don't go overboard!

1 EAT BALANCED MEALS

To ensure you have a balanced diet, try to follow the balanced plate guideline illustrated below for as many of your meals as possible. Whether the foods are separate or mixed together such in a salad or stir-fry, these are the approximate servings you should allocate to each of the food groups.

If you add a fruit and a glass of dairy or soy milk or a yogurt, you will have a nutritious, balanced and filling meal.

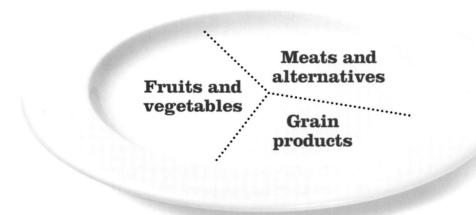

There are other balanced plate models and some devote half the space to vegetables. At Nutrium, the nutrition research center at Université de Montréal, experts recommend filling one-third of your plate with vegetables, mostly because that is a far more realistic goal. Knowing that most people do not eat many vegetables, setting a 50% goal for their plates may be too ambitious, and therefore discouraging. Diets are like sports: it is better to set progressive goals that take into account our current condition. With regard to vegetables, the first step is to include them at each meal. The second step is to allocate one-third of your plate to them. Finally, once you are in the habit, vegetables can take up half your plate. Nevertheless, the breakdown into thirds allows you to ingest more calories, which is an advantage for many athletes.

FRUITS AND VEGETABLES

They can be fresh or frozen, cooked or raw. At breakfast, eat fruits instead of vegetables.

Juices are not a substitute for your fruit and vegetable allotment because they are less nutritious than whole foods. They are less filling because they are swallowed faster than foods, which must be chewed, and are digested more quickly. Moreover, compared to fruits and vegetables, homemade juices prepared with a juicer and especially store-bought juices contain less fiber and vitamins since these nutrients are located in the skin and flesh, which is often removed during the juicing process. Smoothies made with all the parts of the fruit provide a bit more fiber, but are still less filling because they are liquid. The best smoothies are the ones that contain milk, yogurt, soy milk or another good source of protein.

MEAT AND OTHER SOURCES OF PROTEIN

Fish, legumes, chicken, tofu, tempeh, eggs, beef, pork, milk, Greek yogurt and soy milk are excellent sources of protein. Cheese, nuts and seeds contain protein as well, but in less significant quantities; because these foods are very fatty, it is better to rely on them as complementary protein sources rather than primary sources.

GRAIN PRODUCTS

These include bread, couscous, rice, quinoa, millet, barley, buckwheat and pasta. There is a wide array of options. These products may be made with whole grains or refined grains (white bread, white rice, etc.). Ideally, half of the grain products you eat should be whole grains.

2 EAT FILLING FOODS

If you get hungry just an hour or two after a meal, it means that your meal was not filling enough. To feel energized for three or four hours, you need to eat foods that are digested gradually.

The three main elements to consider are protein, dietary fiber and water.

- **INCLUDE A GOOD PROTEIN SOURCE WITH EACH MEAL.** Aim for ½ to 1 oz (15 to 30 g) of protein at breakfast, lunch and dinner. (See "Protein," p. 24.)

- **MAKE A LOT OF ROOM FOR FIBER.** Eat vegetables at lunch and dinner and fruits at breakfast and have at least one fruit as a snack or dessert during the day. Ensure that at least half your bread, cereal, pasta, rice and other grain products are made from whole grains. Eat legumes, nuts, seeds and peanut or nut butters regularly.

- **"EAT" YOUR WATER.** The water contained in foods helps them feel more filling. You can achieve this goal by giving pride of place to fruits and vegetables. A glass of water or juice is never filling. No matter what you think, nothing beats whole fruits and vegetables (see "Fruits and vegetables," p. 33).

The water and fiber found in foods make them heavier and more voluminous, but do not provide any calories. This is an advantage because you are trying to build a full plate and satisfy your taste buds and your stomach while limiting your caloric intake. They are good for everyone, but for those who are watching their weight, these are irreplaceable allies.

3 DRINK ENOUGH WATER

Drink regularly throughout the day. Aim for about 6 cups (1.5 liters) of water and other beverages per day. The best way to check that you are getting enough water is to monitor your urine. If it is abundant and pale (like lemonade), it means you are well hydrated, as opposed to if your urine is dark (except the first time you go in the morning, when urine is always more concentrated).

Begin your day by drinking a tall glass of water. Get into the habit of always having a water bottle or thermos close at hand, at work, when you are on the go and during workouts.

Make water your number one beverage. For variety, add flavor with slices of citrus fruit or a few drops of lemon juice. Use water enhancers sparingly because they are sweetened with sugar substitutes and stoke your taste for sugar. Prepare fruit infusions, which are equally delicious hot or cold.

Limit yourself to ½ to 1 cup (125 to 250 ml) of fruit or vegetable juice per day unless you are an endurance athlete who has trouble meeting your energy needs. Opt for real juices over sweetened beverages or vitamin waters.

Limit yourself to 2 or 3 cups (500 to 750 ml) of coffee per day (see sidebar on p. 57). Try tea or decaffeinated coffee if you tend to drink more than that. When you drink a lot of coffee, caffeine (and theine) works as a diuretic, meaning it boosts your urine production. For this reason and because of all the side effects caused by excessive consumption (e.g. agitation, palpitations, headaches, sleep disruption, irritability), moderation is the rule. If you like flavored coffee beverages, consume them sparingly because they are very sugary.

It is also very important to stay well hydrated during physical activity. (See "Recommendations during exercise," p. 58.)

4 HAVE SNACKS AS NEEDED

Have a snack between meals if you are hungry. It will help you maintain a constant energy level and prevent you from being famished when you sit down to your next meal. It is not wise to wait until you are starving to eat because this generally causes you to eat faster and eat more!

Look at this chart depicting feelings of hunger and satiation. Try to stay between 3 and 5: eat when you are hungry (level 3) and stop eating when you feel just right (level 5).

1.	Starving
2.	Very hungry
3.	**Hungry**
4.	**Somewhat hungry**
5.	**Just right**
6.	Full
7.	Too full

Take advantage of snack times to eat fruits, which are too often neglected at meals.

If you are hungry and your next meal is more than two hours away, include a food rich in fiber or protein in your snack so that it will be filling.

Adapt your choice of snack to the workout you just completed or are about to tackle. Your needs are different before and after a training session. A snack before exercise should deliver energy and be easy to digest, while a snack after exercise should promote recovery. (See "Recommendations before exercise," p. 50 and "Recommendations after exercise," p. 66.)

5 DRINK ALCOHOL IN MODERATION

Alcohol diminishes athletic performance and recovery.
Why? Essentially because:

- Alcohol is metabolized by the liver, which is the same organ that manages how your body uses energy. First, drinking alcohol diminishes glycogen reserves in the liver and, second, it limits the liver's glycogen production (see "Carbohydrates," p. 18).
- Alcohol is a diuretic, so consuming alcohol compromises proper hydration.

Drinking alcohol before and after a workout or competition has several consequences:

- Before (even the night before): Drinking alcohol reduces your energy and water reserves. Result: You are more winded, your heart beats faster and you have less energy. In short, your performance is not as good.
- After: Drinking alcohol slows down recovery and increases the risk of muscle aches.

The idea is not to completely deny yourself the pleasure of drinking alcohol, but simply to manage your consumption better so that it does the least possible damage.

TIPS FOR LIMITING THE DAMAGE CAUSED BY ALCOHOL

- Whenever you drink, make sure you have at least as much water as alcohol. The consequences of alcohol consumption are less serious when you do not have a workout or race in the coming hours because you will have more time to "repair the damage," namely to rehydrate and rebuild your glycogen reserves.

- The best solution is to abstain from alcohol the day before a workout or, especially, a competition. If, however, you drink alcohol, be sure to have two glasses of water per glass of alcohol… and hope that a single drink will satisfy you!

- Eat before or while you consume alcohol.

6 LIMIT CONSUMPTION OF PROCESSED FOODS

Clearly, there are many advantages to eating bars, gels, beverages, chews and other commercially available products for athletes. Their ingredients are specialized and they do not require any preparation. Their packaging is usually convenient and there are a wide variety of choices!

However, it is always possible to replace these processed foods with homemade versions or "regular" food. They also serve the same purpose and are not as costly as the processed versions. Homemade foods give you more knowledge – and therefore more control – of the quality and quantity of ingredients used, not to mention that for some people, preparing your own magic potions gives you a certain sense of satisfaction (but not for everyone, of course!).

The section on foods before, during and after exercise (p. 49) suggests specialized food choices (homemade or commercially produced) and the recipes section (p. 97) will introduce you to solutions that you can prepare on your own in no time.

Food supplements

First of all, you should be aware that food provides everything athletes need to have energy and to build, maintain and repair their muscles. Yes, certain supplements can be useful in specific scenarios, but there is always a catch!

Protein supplements such as **whey** (also known as milk serum proteins) are somewhat helpful when you have to recover quickly from a training session. When combined with carbohydrates, the body absorbs it effectively. That said, you should not under any circumstances replace meat, poultry, eggs, milk and other protein-rich foods with supplements. Foods provide far more than protein, including iron and other important minerals. You should also be warned that "supplements" can quickly become "surplus." Most people get all the protein they need from food. If you have any doubts, consult a sports nutritionist for a needs assessment.

Creatine, an amino acid, may be useful for certain athletes who are trying to increase muscle mass and whose physical efforts are brief and intense. In some cases, it can also promote recovery for endurance athletes when their efforts are intense. You should be extremely careful because creatine sometimes causes gastrointestinal problems and water retention. Furthermore, it is not known whether it is safe for people under the age of 18. Supervision by a healthcare professional is strongly recommended if you want to take creatine because the protocol is complex and tricky.

In conclusion, if you are tempted to take some kind of supplement, have your diet and needs assessed by a sports nutritionist so you can make an informed decision. Another reason to think twice before resorting to supplements is that they may contain illegal substances or contaminants because the food supplement industry is poorly regulated and monitored.

Do not underestimate the power of food. No process can imitate what nature produces. The complexity of food composition and the synergies between their nutrients are impossible to replicate or match...not to mention the pleasure you get from eating them!

7 WATCH OUT FOR DEFICIENCIES IF YOU ARE VEGETARIAN

Depending on the type of vegetarianism you choose, you may have a higher risk of lacking certain types of nutrients. It is absolutely possible to be healthy without eating meat. That said, the more you exclude meat from your diet, the more careful you have to be about not having nutritional deficiencies.

If you are a semi-vegetarian or a flexitarian (occasional vegetarian) and your diet is varied and balanced, you have virtually no risk of dietary deficiencies.

If your diet excludes meat, poultry and fish, but includes eggs, dairy products, legumes, tofu, tempeh, nuts and seeds, then your protein sources are abundant and varied. Still, you should be certain to eat protein at each meal. If you are a lacto-vegetarian or lacto-ovo vegetarian, you must be particularly vigilant in ensuring that you consume enough omega-3 fatty acids and iron, which occur in plant-based foods in lower quantities than in meat and fish. Moreover, the omega-3 fatty acids and iron they contain are not used as effectively by the body as those found in animal-based sources.

If you are a vegan and do not eat any animal product or by-product, you face a bigger challenge. Your protein sources are limited. You have to be imaginative and clever in the kitchen to avoid monotony. You must also be able to plan your meals to avoid deficiencies because sources of omega-3 fatty acids, iron, calcium and vitamins B12 and D are scarcer in a strict vegetarian diet.

WHAT YOU SHOULD KNOW IF YOU DO NOT EAT...

• FISH:

The most beneficial omega-3 fatty acids come from fatty fish. If you do not eat salmon, trout, mackerel, herring, sardines and other such fish, it is important to add flaxseeds, chia seeds or pumpkin seeds to your yogurt, granola, muffins and salads, for example. Add linseed oil to your vinaigrette and use canola oil when you bake muffins, banana bread and other cakes and pastries.

• MEAT, POULTRY, FISH AND SEAFOOD:

These are the best sources of iron because the type of iron they contain (called heme iron) is the kind the body absorbs best compared to the non-heme iron that comes from plants and eggs. Notable sources include lentils, quinoa, spinach and enriched grain products (breakfast cereals, flours, pasta). To help the body absorb and use it better, it is recommended that you include a source of vitamin C (e.g. broccoli, peppers, oranges, strawberries) at the same meal and avoid tea and coffee.

• ANIMAL PRODUCTS AND BY-PROUCTS:

No plant naturally contains B12 in its active form, so if you are vegan, you must consume enriched foods. This includes beverages made from soy, almond, rice or oats, soy-based imitation meats and Brewer's yeast, such as Red Star yeast.

• DAIRY PRODUCTS:

Milk, yogurt and cheese are among the best sources of calcium. Milk and some yogurts are enriched in vitamin D, a vitamin found in few foods. Opt for enriched soy milk because it is the plant-based beverage that most closely resembles milk in terms of calcium, vitamin D and protein. Almond milk and rice milk are good for variety, but they offer less nutritional value.

8 DO NOT OPT FOR A GLUTEN-FREE DIET WITHOUT A MEDICAL REASON

A gluten-free diet is mandatory for people who suffer from celiac disease, but they only make up about 1% of the population. This disease should be diagnosed by a gastroenterologist through blood tests and an intestinal biopsy.

The strong tendency to self-diagnose oneself as gluten intolerant and to adopt a gluten-free diet is harmful. First, this type of diet must be thoroughly explained and taught to ensure that all nutritional needs are met. Second, eliminating gluten complicates – and even compromises – the diagnosis of celiac disease. In fact, blood and intestinal testing can only provide reliable results when there is gluten in your diet. The point is that if you think you may be gluten intolerant, the first step absolutely must be to consult a physician.

A gluten-free diet is restrictive because it eliminates a lot of foods. For this reason, and because many gluten-free products are less nutritious than regular products, you have to plan your diet carefully. Furthermore, you should not overlook how the limitations of a restricted diet will affect your social life.

Gluten-free foods do not have any benefits on your health or athletic performance if you do not need them. That said, embarking on this kind of diet often causes people to improve their eating habits, which means it is not always easy to distinguish the real causes of the patient's well-being.

Gluten is found, in particular, in wheat, barley, spelt, kamut and all their by-products. That includes countless processed foods, in addition to bread, pasta, couscous, bulgur, breakfast cereals, granola bars, baked goods and pastries, pâtés and more. Without a doubt, wheat – and therefore gluten – is found quite frequently in foods. For this simple reason, it is perfectly justifiable, and even wise, to consume a variety of grains. This is why you should include quinoa, buckwheat, rice, corn, rye and millet in your menu. Similar to flexitarians who eat mostly vegetarian dishes, but occasionally have meat, it is possible to open yourself up to new food choices without turning your back on the foods that are part of your regular eating habits.

9 BE DISCIPLINED, BUT DON'T GO OVERBOARD!

It is true that eating well helps you feel stronger and more energetic. In fact, it improves all aspects of sports and exercise. But nutrition is not a religion. Nothing is prohibited and there are no sins or even "lapses." Less nutritious foods can be part of a healthy diet when you eat them occasionally and in reasonable quantities. When you do not allow yourself to eat certain foods, you risk developing a fixation — or even obsession — with them.

Moreover, menus like the ones proposed in the second part of this book (p. 73) and any other recommendations from nutritionists should not become a source of stress. Be flexible in following nutritional advice and do not beat yourself up if you stray from your guidelines, since the sole purpose of such recommendations is to point you in the right direction. They should be adapted to each person and each situation.

Eating should give you pleasure. Eating well tastes good — or at least it should. If that is not yet the case for you, it is simply because you still need to make some adjustments or try some new recipes!

TIPS FOR CHANGING YOUR EATING HABITS

- Introduce changes gradually rather than radically overhauling all your habits.

- Try new cooking methods and a variety of seasonings to pack your food with flavor. No one likes overcooked vegetables that have no taste. The recipes in the third part of this book (p. 97) are here to convince you that eating well tastes good.

- Replace the foods or ingredients you dislike and take the time to learn to enjoy new foods. Your tastes evolve over time.

Before, During and After Exercise

Eating well to have energy all the time is one thing, but eating well to have energy when you are training is another matter. This is where the finer points of sports nutrition come into play.

This section provides you with recommendations that will help you feel energized and ready to begin your workout, keep up the pace and recover effectively.

RECOMMENDATIONS:

1. Recommendations before exercise

2. Recommendations during exercise

3. Recommendations after exercise

1 RECOMMENDATIONS BEFORE EXERCISE

FROM A FEW DAYS TO A FEW MINUTES BEFORE THE EVENT

Your pre-exercise food strategy depends on how much time you have and the type of activity or competition you are preparing for.

Before a major training session or competition, the glycogen reserves in the liver and muscles should be at their maximum capacity (see "Where does energy come from?" p. 14). This is less critical for brief or low-intensity workouts. Your experience also influences your needs. For example, while many athletes can run on an empty stomach in the morning, this is not advisable for inexperienced runners because they might experience discomfort or dizziness.

We will start with how to prepare properly in the days leading up to an endurance event, then go on to how to plan your food intake for the day of the competition, whether you are eating a few minutes before the activity or a few hours before the event or training session.

BASIC GUIDELINES

- **For 2 or 3 days prior to the event:** foods rich in carbohydrates
- **3 to 4 hours before the event:** a normal meal, but with moderate fat content (no fried foods or fatty sauces)
- **1 to 2 hours before the event:** a snack or very light meal that mostly provides carbohydrates, a bit of protein and almost no fat
- **Less than 1 hour before the event:** light snack with carbohydrates

In the days leading up to an endurance event, such as when you are preparing for a competition that will last more than 90 minutes (i.e. long, very long and ultra-long distances), the goal is to load your muscles with glycogen.

Boosting your glycogen reserves is pointless for any physical effort that lasts fewer than 90 minutes. That said, it is still important to eat a carbohydrate-rich diet the day before, as well as a carb-laden meal on the morning of the activity.

The carb-loading protocol can, in theory, be followed for 36 to 48 hours (under two days), but because it requires you to really eat a lot of carbohydrates, the quantities may be unrealistic for some athletes. Building up your glycogen over three days lets you achieve the same result without overburdening the digestive system, so this approach is used more often. The glycogen-loading period usually coincides with a scaled-back training regimen, which encourages your body to retain the glycogen reserves that are being built up. There is no benefit to preceding this phase by fully depleting your reserves.

What constitutes "a lot" of carbohydrates? As part of the three-day glycogen-loading protocol, your target should be at least 7 g per kg of body weight per day. Some studies even suggest aiming for a daily target of 10 to 12 g per kg of body weight. In fact, that is the recommended dose when you are carb-loading over two days. Thus an athlete who weighs 110 lbs (50 kg) should eat at least 350 g (i.e. 50 x 7) of carbohydrates per day for these three days. An athlete who weighs 154 lbs (70 kg) should aim for at least 490 g (i.e. 70 x 7). If your tolerance and experience allow it, try to consume even more. (See "Carbohydrates," p. 18.) Of course, it is strongly recommended that you get personalized advice from a sports nutritionist.

TIPS FOR FILLING UP ON GLYCOGEN IN THE DAYS LEADING UP TO AN ENDURANCE EVENT

- Adjust the food servings on your plate. Instead of having a balanced plate divided into thirds, fill your plate like this:

  ½ plate: pasta, rice, quinoa, potatoes, bread, etc.
  ¼ plate: foods rich in proteins but relatively low in fat
      (e.g. chicken, fish, legumes, tofu)
  ¼ plate: vegetables

- Opt for snacks rich in carbohydrates: muffins, banana bread, fresh or dried fruit, chewy granola bars, flavored yogurt, milk, flavored soy milk, etc.

- It is good to drink more juice than usual, sweeten your coffee, drink chocolate milk, add jam to your toast, and so on. Though it is unwise to make it a habit, adding sugar in moderate amounts is appropriate for these three days.

The menus section contains a three-day regimen for loading up on glycogen (see "Days 17, 18 and 19," pp. 91 to 93), the recipes for which appear in the last part of the book.

3 to 4 hours before a training session or competition, eat a full meal that meets the balanced plate guideline (see "Tips for filling up on glycogen," p. 53). When you are competing or participating in a highly stressful event, it is especially important to choose somewhat bland foods that are easy for you to digest and do not contain too much fat or fiber. Digestive discomfort is more common when you feel nervous. Above all – and this is the most important tip – only eat foods to which you are accustomed. Event days should never be a time to try something new!

1 to 2 hours before a training session or competition, have a snack. If you exercise at lunchtime or after work, your most recent meal may not be enough to sustain you when you work out. Similarly, if you have an event that starts in the morning, you should eat when you wake up. Here are some ideas:

- 1 Green Smoothie (p. 134)
- 1 slice of toast with jam or peanut butter
- 1 small bowl of cereal with yogurt or milk
- 1 Chewy Bar (p. 128) and 1 fruit
- 1 Blueberry Hazelnut Muffin (p. 122) and 1 glass of juice
- Crackers and hummus
- ½ chicken sandwich

WHERE DOES HYDRATION FIT IN?

Drinking water regularly throughout the day should be part of your routine. Keep water within reach at work and when you are on the go. From a few hours to a few minutes before your training session or competition, hydration is another critical factor. Drink 2 cups (500 ml) of water about two hours before the event. This will give you time to eliminate any excess water before it becomes inconvenient to do so. Then, take small sips as your thirst dictates until the event begins.

Less than 1 hour before a training session or competition, you can eat something light that will not weigh down your stomach and that will digest quickly to give you energy fast. If, for example, you work out early in the morning, you probably do not want to get up too much in advance in order to have breakfast. Here are some suggested foods that you can eat up to a few minutes before lacing up your running shoes:

- 1 glass of juice diluted with water
- 1 sports beverage
- 1 (or ½) banana
- 2 or 3 dried apricots
- 1 Chewy Bar (p. 128)
- 1 fig cookie
- 1 fruit yogurt if this works for you (some athletes do not tolerate protein before exercise)

BEET JUICE AND COFFEE

Of course, all athletes should avoid prohibited performance-enhancing substances. But why shy away from foods that can help you perform better? Some athletes, for example, consume beet juice and coffee.

BEET JUICE

In some cases, consuming beet juice can have a slight impact on performance. Studies conducted on a small number of highly trained athletes showed a performance improvement of approximately 2% with regards to speed of execution or power generated.

Beet juice is very rich in nitrates. Once ingested, the nitrates are converted to nitrites, then to nitrogen oxide in the body. This increased concentration of nitrogen oxide in the blood appears to assist endurance training by helping the muscles perform better, in particular by requiring less oxygen for a given effort.

The study protocols varied, ranging from 2 cups (500 ml) of beet juice per day for 6 days to 2 cups (500 ml) taken just once, 2.5 hours before the physical test. The results are still not conclusive, but what seems clear is that there is a spike in the nitrogen oxide concentration in the blood 2.5 hours after drinking the beet juice. Therefore, whether you drink it for six days or just once, the optimal lead time for the last dose is 2.5 hours before the sports event. However, it is not recommended that you start gulping beet juice as if it were a magic potion because little is known about the long-term effects of consuming large quantities. Remember that nitrites are associated with the development of certain types of cancer, so proceed with caution. To sum up, more studies are needed to rule on the effectiveness and safety of consuming vast amounts of beet juice.

COFFEE

It is likely that caffeine improves performance during endurance sports practiced at medium or high intensity. It seems to help reduce one's perception of pain and to improve muscle effort if consumed before or during exercise. The effective dose appears to be 2.3 mg of caffeine per lb (5 mg per kg) body weight, or 350 mg for an athlete who weighs 154 lbs (70 kg). That comes out to about 2 cups (500 ml) of drip coffee. The studies primarily used caffeine tablets because their caffeine content is easier to gauge than that of a cup of coffee. It is important to be aware of your own tolerance for caffeine and not to go beyond the suggested dose: if coffee causes you uneasiness, palpitations, accelerated breathing or headaches, you will not derive a net benefit. You should also be mindful of how much liquid this represents. Drinking 2 cups (500 ml) of coffee 1 hour before your event (recommended dose) could become an inconvenience just before you begin exercising.

2 RECOMMENDATIONS DURING EXERCISE

What you should drink and eat while you are exercising depends on the duration and intensity of the effort.

WHEN EXERCISING FOR LESS THAN 1 HOUR

SPECIFIC NEED: water

WHAT YOU SHOULD DRINK: a few sips of water every 15 to 20 minutes

WHAT YOU SHOULD EAT: nothing in particular

Nevertheless, some studies suggest that for high-intensity sports that last 45 to 75 minutes, rinsing your mouth with a sugary beverage or swallowing a very small amount of this beverage could be helpful.

WHEN EXERCISING FOR 1 TO 2 HOURS

SPECIFIC NEEDS: water, carbohydrates and maybe electrolytes (see sidebar, p. 61)

WHAT YOU SHOULD DRINK: a few sips of water or sports beverage every 15 to 20 minutes

Sports beverages contain a small amount of carbohydrates (about 6 to 8 g per ⅓ cup/80 ml) that can be absorbed rapidly. It is also easy to prepare a homemade sports drink using the juice of your choice. Simply mix equal amounts of juice and water and add two pinches of salt per 4 cups (1 liter).

The most important thing is to enjoy the flavor of your beverage because that will motivate you to drink it. If sugar does not agree with you, note that maltodextrin-based beverages are an effective fuel source, but their flavor is far less pronounced. And, of course, there is always water.

Drink 1½ to 3¼ cups (375 to 800 ml) of sports beverage per hour so as to get 30 to 60 g of carbohydrates per hour. This is roughly equivalent to an average-sized water bottle. Drink the amount that feels right to you. Let your thirst be your guide so you avoid over-hydrating or feeling bloated. If the recommended amount of fluid is unrealistic for you, use foods to achieve the ideal dose of carbohydrates.

WHAT YOU SHOULD EAT: it depends!

If you cannot reach the minimum recommended amount of carbohydrates with a sports drink, or if you prefer water, eat something sweet. Whether it is a specialized, commercially available product, a homemade recipe or a non-processed food, begin eating within the first 15 to 20 minutes of activity to avoid a drop in energy and performance. Most importantly, do not wait until you feel weak to eat. Then continue snacking every 15 to 20 minutes.

Suggested foods that provide approximately 30 g of carbohydrates:

- 1 banana
- 5 dates
- 2 fruit jellies
- 1 energy bar with fruit
- 2 fig cookies
- 2 Chews (p. 124)
- 1 packet of energy gel

ELECTROLYTES

Perspiration is salty. The salts it contains are called electrolytes. These are mainly comprised of sodium and potassium, though there is far more sodium in perspiration than potassium. If you perspire profusely for 3, 4, 5 or more hours, it is critical that you replace the salt you lose. A lack of sodium in the blood (hyponatremia) can cause an accelerated heart rate, nausea, vomiting, headaches, confusion and even convulsions. Simply put, it is dangerous.

Hydration drinks for athletes contain some sodium and potassium. There are also electrolyte solutions in powder or liquid form that can be added to water or a hydration beverage. They usually contain a more diverse blend of electrolytes. Nevertheless, you should remember that sodium is the most important element to replenish. So if you prepare a homemade hydration beverage, just add table salt. Adding this sodium is enough to fulfill your electrolyte needs during long training sessions or competitions. The recommended quantity is about ¼ tsp per 4 cups (1 liter), which provides 500 to 700 g of sodium.

Do electrolytes prevent cramps? They seem to be part of the equation, though definitive evidence is lacking. Cramps remain one of the least understood aspects of sports and exercise.

WHEN EXERCISING FOR MORE THAN 2 HOURS

SPECIFIC NEEDS: water, carbohydrates and electrolytes (see sidebar, p. 61)

WHAT YOU SHOULD DRINK: same as when you exercise for 1 to 2 hours (see p. 60). If you sweat a lot and for an extended period, add electrolytes to your water or beverage. Drinks made with maltodextrin, which has a neutral flavor, can also be useful if you do not want something that tastes sweet.

To find out whether your hydration strategy is sufficient, weigh yourself before and after a training session that simulates a competition. Any weight loss over the workout is water. Each 2.2 lbs (1 kilo) you lose corresponds to a water deficit of 4 cups (1 liter). You lose between 1½ and 7¼ cups (375 ml and 1.8 liters) of sweat per hour, which means it is impossible for athletes who perspire profusely to make up 100% of their losses. The goal is not to be more than 2% dehydrated. For an athlete who weighs 154 lbs (70 kg), that would amount to 3 lbs (1.4 kg) in weight. If your water loss is greater than 2%, you must revise your hydration strategy. The goal is to find the right balance between quenching your thirst and avoiding a bloated sensation.

WHAT YOU SHOULD EAT: 30 to 60 g of carbohydrates per hour

However, because it is virtually certain that you will get sick of sweet flavors, it is wise to plan on neutral, or even salty, foods that provide carbohydrates (e.g. pita bread, bagel, rice crackers, baked corn chips – the originals have too much fat).

OVER 2.5 HOURS IS A REAL CHALLENGE!

When you exercise for more than 2.5 hours, it is recommended that you eat up to 90 g of carbohydrates per hour, which is a challenge in itself. Ultra-endurance athletes who run 80, 125, 160 km or more do not limit themselves to sugary beverages and foods. They have very specific needs. These athletes expend more energy than seems natural and they lose liters of fluids through perspiration, in addition to the fact that they often run at night and in the cold. Although they carry drinks and some food with them, they rely on several refueling stations along the course. The foods offered at these stations include potatoes, gnocchi, sports bars, soup, fruit, chews, chocolate candies, chips and carbonated beverages. At first glance, this defies all logic, but there is an explanation.

First, ultra-competitors (let's call them "the machines") have to eat calorie-dense foods to compensate for their tremendous energy expenditure. Fat is the food component that contains the most calories, so they go for it! Second, over time, ultrarunners develop their ability to use a larger serving of lipids (fats) as fuel. Third, to prevent boredom, athletes must consume a variety of flavors and textures. It would be unbearable to get all your energy from sports drinks and sweet bars.

Sodas are still not recommended for all athletes, especially because their high sugar concentration slows absorption of the fluid and the carbon dioxide can cause digestive discomfort. But for runners, the fact that the beverage stays in the stomach for a long time is not critical because they will still be exerting themselves when the energy becomes available. Furthermore, some runners feel a sense of lightness when they release the gas (or burp, if you prefer). Anything that helps you feel comfortable is precious during these superhuman endeavors.

EVERY SPORT HAS SPECIAL CONSIDERATIONS

Energy and water needs, as well as the kind of food or drink you can consume during exercise, are different depending on the sport. Runners are able to withstand a lot, but their digestive systems are somewhat unpredictable.

During exercise, your muscles are the priority destination for blood and oxygen, not your stomach. Moreover, your body's position and movements during exercise also influence your tolerance for certain foods. The movements associated with running cause a lot of upheaval. Stride after stride, you are shaking things up! When you cycle, your position compresses the stomach and intestines. For swimmers, the horizontal position and flips and turns interfere with digestion. There are specific concerns for every sport. These are some of the reasons you should base what, when and how much you eat on your sport and your own body's tolerance. If you do not take these precautions, gastrointestinal problems await! Stitches, sluggishness, stomachaches, acid reflux (when food "comes back up"), bathroom emergencies...you are bound to be familiar with at least some of these side effects.

As you apply the basic principles of sports nutrition, you should continue to learn about yourself. There is always a bit of trial and error when it comes to figuring out what suits you best. This is why it is crucial to learn your lessons when you are training and not when you are competing or participating in events.

3 RECOMMENDATIONS AFTER EXERCISE

What you should eat after exercising depends on the type of activity. The answer could very well be "nothing special." If you swam, ran or biked for 30 minutes, a post-workout snack is not essential. And if you are watching your weight, it might just be too much. Overestimating your energy expenditure (see p. 12) and overcompensating by eating more is a common mistake. The hard and fast rule is that you should eat a snack if you are hungry, as you normally would, and not because you think that your workout requires that you eat more.

Your physical effort should be sufficiently long – at least 60 to 90 minutes – and intense to deem a post-workout snack necessary. If this is the case, and especially if you train for over two hours, you should optimize your recovery. Indeed, two hours of hard exercise depletes the glycogen reserves in the liver and muscles, causes significant water loss, tears muscle fiber, damages red blood cells and weakens the immune system. So this is the time for food that promotes cell repair and the rebuilding of energy reserves. This is all the more important if your next training session is less than 24 hours away. Without an appropriate diet, you will not make a complete recovery and your performance will be less than ideal.

WHEN? No more than 30 minutes after exercise.

You will recover faster if you eat within this time frame. During this period, the cells in your body throw their doors wide open to take in everything you can give them. You should seize this opportunity because after 30 minutes, it is less effective.

If your workout was particularly long and intense, a single snack within 30 minutes will not suffice. You have to eat a small meal one hour later and, in extreme cases, every hour for several hours, otherwise you will feel tired for a longer time.

WHAT? Foods that give you carbohydrates, protein, water and electrolytes.

Carbohydrates rebuild the glycogen reserves in your liver and muscles and promote protein use by damaged muscles (for muscle repair). Water replenishes the fluids lost through sweat and helps store glycogen. Electrolytes also offset the losses suffered during exercise.

Solid foods can encourage recovery, but there are various reasons to select fluids instead. First, they accomplish two goals at once because they are digested more quickly and they provide water. Second, if you tend not to have much of an appetite right after a big training session, you will undoubtedly be more inclined to drink than to eat something.

HOW MUCH? After a long, exhausting and strenuous training workout that has pushed your muscles to the brink, it is recommended that you aim for 0.45 to 0.7 g of carbohydrates per pound of body weight (1 to 1.5 g/kg body weight) and 0.1 to 0.18 g of protein per pound of body weight (0.2 to 0.4 g/kg body weight) if you are an athlete who trains every day. If, for example, you weigh 154 lbs (70 kg), that means 70 to 107 g of carbohydrates and 15 to 27 g of protein.

If you are a diligent athlete but you spread your workout over four (or sometimes five) days a week, you will require fewer carbohydrates after a strenuous workout lasting over 90 minutes: approximately 30 g is enough. You should still try to get 14 to 28 g of protein.

After training for 60 to 90 minutes, a snack that provides 30 g of carbohydrates and about 10 g of protein is fine.

RECOMMENDATIONS AFTER EXERCISE

- After an intense training session lasting 60 to 90 minutes

- After a strenuous, exhausting training session if no other workout is planned in the immediate future

- After a strenuous, exhausting training session if another workout is planned within the next 24 hours

After an intense training session lasting 60 to 90 minutes		
FOOD	CARBOHYDRATE CONTENT (in g)	PROTEIN CONTENT (in g)
Yellow Smoothie (p. 127)	32	10
1 cup (250 ml) fruit yogurt	30	10
Watermelon + 1 cup (250 ml) flavored soy milk	35	8
1 smoothie made from 1 cup (250 ml) milk + 1 cup (250 ml) frozen raspberries	30	11
1 serving Chocolate Pudding (p. 118)	41	12
½ bagel + 2 tbsp peanut butter	26	12
Crackers + 1 oz (30 g) hummus + 1 oz (30 g) cheese + 1 cup (250 ml) vegetable juice	30	15

After a strenuous, exhausting training session if no other workout is planned in the immediate future

FOOD	CARBOHYDRATE CONTENT (in g)	PROTEIN CONTENT (in g)
Red Smoothie (p. 138)	30	27
1 cup (250 ml) Greek yogurt with strawberries	30	20
1 cup (250 ml) chocolate milk + 1 cup (250 ml) plain milk	39	16
1 cup (250 ml) chicken noodle soup + 1 small pita bread + ½ cup (125 ml) pieces of cooked chicken	28	30

After a strenuous, exhausting training session if another workout is planned within the next 24 hours

FOOD	CARBOHYDRATE CONTENT (in g)	PROTEIN CONTENT (in g)
Red Smoothie (p. 138) + 1 bagel	70	35
1 cup (250 ml) Greek yogurt with strawberries + 1 banana + 1 cup (250 ml) fruit juice (or a smoothie made from these three ingredients)	90	20
1 cup (250 ml) chocolate milk + 1 cup (250 ml) plain milk + 1 muffin + 1 orange	80	22
1 cup (250 ml) chicken noodle soup + 1 large pita bread + ½ cup (125 ml) pieces of cooked chicken + 1 cup (250 ml) fruit juice	75	30

SUMMARY CHARTS

BEFORE A WORKOUT	SAMPLE FOODS	NOTES
1 to 3 days before	Full meal (with pasta, bread or rice, for example) + water, tea, juice, etc.	
3 to 4 hours before	Full meal (balanced plate) + water	Relatively bland foods that are easy for you to digest and do not contain too much fat or fiber
1 to 2 hours before	Chewy Bar (p. 128) + fruit + water **OR** Homemade muffin + juice	
Less than 1 hour before	2 or 3 dried apricots + water **OR** Juice diluted with water	

DURING A WORKOUT	SAMPLE FOODS	NOTES
Exercise for less than 1 hour	Water	A few sips every 15 to 20 minutes
Exercise for 1 to 2 hours	Dates + water and/or sports drinks **OR** 2 Chews (p. 124)	
Exercise for more than 2 hours	Sports bar + water and/or sports drink **OR** Pita bread + water and/or sports drink	A few sips or mouthfuls of food every 15 to 20 minutes
Exercise for more than 2.5 hours	Banana, bagel, chicken noodle soup + water and/or sports drink	

AFTER EXERCISE	SAMPLE FOODS	NOTES
Exercise for 60 to 90 minutes	Chocolate Pudding (p. 118) + water **OR** Yellow Smoothie (p. 127) + water **OR** Bread with peanut butter + water	Eat within 30 minutes of completing your workout. Drink until your urine is pale in color.
Exercise for 1 to 2 hours	Red Smoothie (p. 138) + water **OR** Greek yogurt with fruit + water **OR** Soup + bread + chicken + water	Eat within 30 minutes of completing your workout. Eat again one hour later. Drink until your urine is pale in color.
Exhausting training session with another workout planned within the next 24 hours	Red Smoothie (p. 138) + bagel + water **OR** Greek yogurt with fruit + banana + juice + water **OR** Store-bought chocolate milk (diluted with half regular milk) + muffin + orange + water	Eat within 30 minutes of completing your workout. Eat again once an hour for several hours. Drink until your urine is pale in color.

21 DAYS
OF MENUS

The menus in this book were developed to provide you with all the nutrients and energy you need to stay in shape each day. We have designed menus to accommodate workouts at different times of the day so that you can plan what you eat before, during and after exercising. Adapt these suggestions to your schedule and personal situation.

Servings and quantities are not provided because that depends on you. Every person's needs are unique. Eat to satisfy your hunger. Enjoy, eliminate or supplement the suggested snacks as needed. You can also have them as a dessert if you are still hungry at the end of a meal. Feel free to draw inspiration from the recipes in this book to find snacks that you enjoy. The same goes for the accompanying vegetables: choose the ones that you like, but be sure to include some vegetables with every lunch and dinner.

You will notice that the suggested lunches are often leftovers from the previous evening's dinner. This means you may have to double or triple the servings in the recipe so that you have leftovers the next day.

As you plan your week, get ideas from the suggested menus and make a grocery list to buy all the ingredients needed to prepare the recipes.

WEEKS 1 and 2: Regular workouts (at different times of day)	
WEEK 3: Before, during and after a sporting event	

DAY 1

BREAKFAST

Granola #1 (p. 98)
Milk, soy milk or yogurt

Snack
Energy Balls (p. 117)

⏱ 45 to 60 minute workout

LUNCH

Savory Rice Balls (p. 140)
Hard-boiled eggs
Raw vegetables
Cheese

Snack
Chocolate Pudding (p. 118)

DINNER

Chicken Pizza (p. 142)
Green salad

Snack
Pineapple Strawberry Salad (p. 120)

DAY 2

BREAKFAST ....

Toasted bread with Mocha Hazelnut Spread (p. 100)
Milk, soy milk or coffee with milk

Snack
Fresh fruit

LUNCH ....

Chicken Pizza (p. 142)
Raw vegetables

Snack
Chocolate Pudding (p.118)

DINNER ....

Crispy Tofu with Broccoli (p. 144)
Rice

Snack
Blueberry Hazelnut Muffins (p. 122)

DAY 3

BREAKFAST

Lumberjack Pancakes (p. 102)
Milk, soy milk or coffee with milk

Snack Fresh fruit	

LUNCH

Herring alla Puttanesca (p. 147)
Green salad

Snack Savory Rice Balls (p. 140)	

⏱ 60 to 75 minute workout

DINNER

Quick Couscous with Black Beans
and Vegetables (p. 148)

Snack Pineapple Strawberry Salad (p. 120)	

DAY 4

BREAKFAST

Oatmeal to Go (p. 104)

> **Snack**
> Fresh fruit
>

LUNCH

Crispy Tofu with Broccoli (p. 144)
Rice

> **Snack**
> Chocolate Pudding (p. 118)
>

DINNER

Beet Patties (p. 150)
Edamame Purée (p. 152)
Choice of bread

> **Snack**
> Yogurt with berries and Granola
> (p. 98 or p. 112)
>

DAY 5

BREAKFAST

Coffee Energy Bars (p. 106)
Greek yogurt

Snack
Rice crackers and hummus

⏱ 45 to 60 minute workout

LUNCH

Beet Patties (p. 150)
Edamame Purée (p. 152)
Choice of bread

Snack
Energy Balls (p. 117)

DINNER

Chicken Drumsticks with Polenta (p. 154)
Sautéed snow peas

Snack
Applesauce

DAY 6

BREAKFAST

Muesli (p. 109)

Snack
During workout: Chews (p. 124)
After workout: Yellow Smoothie (p. 127)

⏱ 90 to 120 minute workout

LUNCH

White Bean and Sautéed Vegetable Wraps (p. 157)
Raw vegetables

Snack
Fresh fruit
Cheese

DINNER

Honey Mustard Arctic Char (p. 158)
Orzo with Parmesan cheese

Snack
Applesauce

DAY 7

BREAKFAST . . . .

Breakfast Couscous (p. 110)

Snack Fresh fruit	

LUNCH . . . .

Hearty Legume Soup (p. 160)

Snack Blueberry Hazelnut Muffins (p. 122)	

DINNER . . . .

Pan-Fried White Beans with Creamed Spinach (p. 162)
Choice of bread

Snack Yogurt with or without Granola (p. 98 or p. 112)	

DAY 8

BREAKFAST ·

Toast with Mocha Hazelnut Spread (p. 100)
Milk, soy milk or coffee with milk

Snack
Fresh fruit

LUNCH ·

Farfalle Salad with Arctic Char (p. 164)

Snack
Chewy Bars (p. 128)

⏱ 60 to 75 minute workout

DINNER ·

Pork and Mint Vermicelli (p.167)

Snack
Fresh fruit

DAY 9

BREAKFAST

Granola #2 (p. 112)
Milk, soy milk or yogurt

Snack
Fresh fruit

LUNCH

Pan-Fried White Beans with Creamed Spinach (p. 162)
Choice of bread

Snack
Sweet Rice Balls (p. 130)

DINNER

Coffee Energy Bars (p. 106)

⏱ 60 to 75 minute workout

Late dinner
Omelet in a Cup (p. 168)
Sautéed frozen vegetables
Choice of bread

DAY 10

BREAKFAST

Coffee Energy Bars (p. 106)
Greek yogurt

Snack
Fresh fruit

LUNCH

Pork and Mint Vermicelli (p. 167)

Snack
Applesauce and Granola #2 (p. 112)

DINNER

Chicken Fried Rice (p. 170)
Green salad

Snack
Brownie in a Cup (p. 132)

DAY 11

BREAKFAST

Breakfast Couscous (p. 110)

Snack
Green Smoothie (p. 134)

⏱ 45 to 60 minute workout

LUNCH

Hearty Legume Soup (p. 160)

Snack
Chewy Bars (p. 128)

DINNER

Rice Noodles with Smoked Oysters (p. 172)
Sautéed bok choy

Snack
Yogurt with berries and Granola
(p. 98 or p. 112)

DAY 12

BREAKFAST . . . .

Breakfast Drink (p. 114)
Diluted orange juice
Dried apricots

Snack
Coffee Energy Bars (p. 106)

LUNCH . . . .

Chicken Fried Rice (p. 170)
Green salad

Snack
Fresh fruit

DINNER . . . .

Vegetarian Banh Mi (p. 174)
Grated carrot salad

Snack
Energy Balls (p. 117)

DAY 13

BREAKFAST

Muesli (p. 109)

⏱ Workout over 90 minutes

During workout: Chews (p. 124)

Snack
Yellow Smoothie (p. 127)

LUNCH

Herring alla Puttanesca (p. 147)
Green salad

Snack
Brownie in a Cup (p. 132)

DINNER

Star Anise Blade Steak (p. 177)

Snack
Pineapple Strawberry Salad (p. 120)

DAY 14

BREAKFAST

Toast with Mocha Hazelnut Spread (p. 100)
Milk, soy milk or coffee with milk

Snack
Pineapple Strawberry Salad (p. 120)

LUNCH

Vegetarian Banh Mi (p. 174)
Vegetable soup

Snack
Tortilla Chips (p. 137)

DINNER

Salmon Cubes and Quinoa (p. 178)
Tomato and cucumber salad

Snack
Applesauce and Granola
(p. 98 or p. 112)

DAY 15

BREAKFAST

Diluted fruit juice

⏱ 45 to 60 minute workout

Oatmeal to Go (p. 104)

Snack
Fresh fruit
Cheese

LUNCH

Salmon Cubes and Quinoa (p. 178)
Tomato and cucumber salad

Snack
Chocolate Pudding (p. 118)

DINNER

Gemelli Carbonara (p. 180)
Green beans

Snack
Yogurt

DAY 16

BREAKFAST ....

Coffee Energy Bars (p. 106)
Greek yogurt

Snack
Fresh fruit

LUNCH ....

Shredded Beef Sandwiches
with Napa Cabbage Salad (p. 182)

Vegetable soup

Snack
Sweet Rice Balls (p. 130)

⏱ 60 to 75 minute workout

DINNER ....

Pesto Couscous (p. 184)

Snack
Applesauce and Granola
(p. 98 or p. 112)

DAY 17

BREAKFAST

Orange juice
Bagel with Mocha Hazelnut Spread (p. 100)
Milk, soy milk or coffee with milk

Snack
Fresh fruit
Chewy Bars (p. 128)
Chocolate milk or flavored soy milk

LUNCH

Gemelli Carbonara (p. 180)
Broccoli cooked in microwave
Muffins
Fruit yogurt

Snack
Tortilla Chips (p. 137)
Salsa
Fruit juice

DINNER

Shrimp and Squash Risotto (p. 187)
Baguette bread
Green salad
Brownie in a Cup (p. 132)
Milk or soy milk

Snack
Oatmeal cookies
Banana

DAY 18

BREAKFAST ....

Orange juice
Breakfast Couscous (p. 110)

> **Snack**
> Chewy Bars (p. 128)
> Fruit juice

LUNCH ....

Curried Tofu Salad Sandwiches (p. 188)
Raw vegetables
Fruit yogurt
Energy Balls (p. 117)

> **Snack**
> Fresh fruit
> Rice crackers
> Milk or flavored soy milk

DINNER ....

Salmon and Dill Spaghetti (p. 190)
Baguette bread
Steamed or sautéed broccoli
Date square
Fruit juice

> **Snack**
> Yogurt with Granola (p. 98 or p. 112)
> Banana

DAY 19

BREAKFAST ....

Breakfast Drink (p. 114)

⏱ 20 minute workout

Snack
Energy Balls (p. 117)
Milk or soy milk

LUNCH ....

Salmon and Dill Spaghetti (p. 190)
Vegetable juice
Oatmeal cookies

Snack
Chewy Bars (p. 128)
Fresh fruit
Fruit juice

DINNER ....

Shrimp and Squash Risotto (p. 187)
Baguette bread
Green salad
Chocolate Pudding (p. 118)

Snack
Banana
Muffins
Flavored soy milk

DAY 20

BREAKFAST

Your usual breakfast (e.g. oatmeal, toast or bagel with peanut butter or jelly, cereal)

🏆 Major training session or competition: over 90 minutes

Chews (p. 124)

> **Snack**
> Red Smoothie (p. 138)
> Bagel

LUNCH

Meal provided at event or Farfalle Salad with Arctic Char (p. 164)

> **Snack**
> Tortilla Chips (p. 137)
> Fresh fruit

DINNER

Chicken Pizza (p. 142)
Cherry tomato salad

> **Snack**
> Brownie in a Cup (p. 132)
> Milk or soy milk

DAY 21

BREAKFAST

Omelet in a Cup (p. 168)
Whole-grain bread

Snack
Fresh fruit
Cheese

LUNCH

Pork and Mint Vermicelli (p. 167)
Sautéed frozen vegetables

Snack
Coffee Energy Bars (p. 106)

DINNER

Pesto Couscous (p. 184)

Snack
Yogurt with Granola
(p. 98 or p. 112)

RECISPES
47 HEALTHY IDEAS

If we could, we would add several hours to your day to give you time to cook without feeling rushed. Instead, we have compiled a collection of recipes that are quick and easy to prepare. They will give you energy for your athletic activities and for your daily undertakings. Some of the recipes feature "SPORTS INFO" boxes that recap some of the information provided in the first section of this book.

On your marks, get set, cook!

GRANOLA

#1

14 servings • PREPARATION: 10 minutes • COOKING TIME: 30 minutes

INGREDIENTS

4 cups (1 l) old-fashioned rolled oats (not instant)

¾ cup (180 ml) almonds

¼ cup (60 ml) ground flaxseed

½ cup (125 ml) maple syrup

¼ cup (60 ml) butter, melted

2 tsp ground cinnamon

½ tsp salt

¾ cup (180 ml) raisins

Nutrition Facts	
For ½ cup (125 ml)	
Amount	
Calories	247 kcal
Fat	11 g
Sodium	89 mg
Carbohydrate	34 g
Fiber	4 g
Protein	6 g

METHOD

Position rack in middle of oven and preheat to 300°F (150°C). Line a baking sheet with parchment paper.

In a bowl, combine all ingredients except raisins. Spread onto prepared baking sheet and cook in middle of preheated oven, for 30 minutes, stirring halfway through cooking.

Remove mixture from oven and add raisins and stir.

• • • • • • • • • • • • •

VARIATION

For variety, you can replace the almonds with other nuts or seeds, and the raisins with other dried fruit (e.g. pecans and cranberries, pistachios and apricots).

• • • • • • • • • • • • •

TIPS

• Serve the granola with yogurt, applesauce, milk or soy milk. It is also delicious with fresh fruit.

• Dried fruit should only be added after baking since it burns easily.

• The granola can be stored in an airtight container at room temperature for up to 6 months.

MOCHA HAZELNUT
Spread

15 servings • PREPARATION: 10 minutes

INGREDIENTS

⅓ cup (80 ml) cocoa powder

⅓ cup (80 ml) strong hot coffee

1 cup (250 ml) hazelnut butter

¼ cup (60 ml) maple syrup

METHOD

In a food processor, combine cocoa powder and coffee. Scrape down sides.

Add hazelnut butter and maple syrup. Pulse for about 30 seconds. Scrape sides then pulse again for 30 seconds.

• • • • • • • • • • • • •

TIP

The spread can be stored in an airtight container in the refrigerator for up to 1 month.

Nutrition Facts For 2 tbsp	
Amount	
Calories	205 kcal
Fat	18 g
Sodium	4 mg
Carbohydrate	9 g
Fiber	3 g
Protein	4 g

LUMBERJACK
Pancakes

12 pancakes • PREPARATION: 15 minutes • COOKING TIME: 20 minutes

INGREDIENTS

1 cup (250 ml) whole wheat flour

1 tsp baking powder

¼ tsp baking soda

Pinch salt

½ cup (125 ml) millet

3 tbsp ground almonds

¼ tsp ground cinnamon

1 egg, beaten

1 cup (250 ml) 2% milk

1 tsp vanilla extract

METHOD

In a large bowl, combine flour, baking powder, baking soda, salt, millet, almonds and cinnamon.

In another bowl, whisk egg, milk and vanilla. Pour into bowl with flour preparation and stir.

Lightly grease a nonstick skillet with canola oil and heat over medium heat. Drop about 3 tbsp of batter on skillet to form a 4-inch (10 cm) pancake. Cook for 2 to 3 minutes until bubbles begin to form on surface. Turn pancake over with a spatula and cook for 2 to 3 minutes. Repeat for each pancake.

. . . .

TIPS

- A 12-inch (30 cm) skillet can be used to cook three pancakes at once.

- The pancakes can be stored in an airtight container in the refrigerator for 3 or 4 days. They are easy to transport.

SPORTS INFO

The pancakes fit easily in a running backpack and make a good post-workout snack for workouts lasting over 90 minutes.

Nutrition Facts For 3 pancakes	
Amount	
Calories	353 kcal
Fat	13 g
Sodium	229 mg
Carbohydrate	46 g
Fiber	6 g
Protein	13 g

OATMEAL
to Go

1 serving • PREPARATION: 5 minutes • COOKING TIME: 2 minutes

INGREDIENTS

⅓ cup (80 ml) quick-cooking rolled oats

⅓ cup (80 ml) water

⅓ cup (80 ml) 2% milk

1 tbsp maple syrup or brown sugar

⅔ cup (160 ml) Greek yogurt, plain

⅓ cup (80 ml) frozen blueberries

METHOD

In a microwave-safe bowl, combine rolled oats, water and milk. Cook in microwave for 60 to 90 seconds (monitor cooking time, because oatmeal expands and can overflow).

Let rest for several minutes then transfer to an airtight container (e.g. 2-cup/500 ml Mason jar). Add maple syrup, yogurt and blueberries (use caution if handling bottom of container, as it may be very hot).

• • • • • • • • • • • • •

VARIATION

This portable oatmeal is particularly convenient for early-morning workouts. It can be prepared very quickly and can be eaten post-workout, on the move or at work.

Nutrition Facts
Per serving

Amount	
Calories	342 kcal
Fat	4 g
Sodium	108 mg
Carbohydrate	53 g
Fiber	6 g
Protein	24 g

COFFEE
Energy Bars

12 bars • PREPARATION: 10 minutes • COOKING TIME: 5 minutes • REFRIGERATION: 4 hours

INGREDIENTS

½ cup (125 ml) almond butter

½ cup (125 ml) strong coffee

½ cup (125 ml) maple syrup

2 cups (500 ml) quick-cooking rolled oats

1 cup (250 ml) almonds, coarsely ground, or almond powder

½ cup (125 ml) dried apricots or apples, coarsely chopped

METHOD

Line a 9-inch (23 cm) square pan with parchment paper.

In a saucepan over medium-high heat, whisk almond butter, coffee and maple syrup for 5 minutes until smooth.

In a large bowl, combine rolled oats, almonds and dried fruit. Using a wooden spoon, incorporate liquid mixture.

Pour mixture into prepared pan and press down firmly. Refrigerate for 4 hours prior to cutting into 12 bars.

• • • • • • • • • • • • • •

TIP

The bars can be stored in an airtight container in the refrigerator for up to 7 days or in an airtight bag in the freezer for up to 3 months.

Nutrition Facts	
Per bar	
Amount	
Calories	218 kcal
Fat	12 g
Sodium	4 mg
Carbohydrate	23 g
Fiber	4 g
Protein	7 g

2 servings • PREPARATION: 5 minutes • REFRIGERATION: overnight

METHOD

In a bowl, combine rolled oats, yogurt and milk. Cover and refrigerate overnight.

Add apple, banana, raisins and maple syrup. Mix well.

• • • • • • • • • • • • •

VARIATION

Use seasonal fruit. In the summer, enjoy the many berries and stone fruits (e.g. peaches, nectarines, apricots) available. Apples are particularly tasty in the fall, and winter is ideal for citrus fruit.

• • • • • • • • • • • • •

TIP

The muesli can be carried in a Mason jar or any other airtight container.

INGREDIENTS

⅔ cup (160 ml) quick-cooking rolled oats

¾ cup (180 ml) Greek yogurt, plain

1 cup (250 ml) 2% milk

1 green apple (Granny Smith), diced

1 banana, sliced

2 tbsp raisins

1 tbsp maple syrup

Nutrition Facts Per serving	
Amount	
Calories	348 kcal
Fat	5 g
Sodium	99 mg
Carbohydrate	60 g
Fiber	6 g
Protein	18 g

Couscous

2 servings • PREPARATION: 10 minutes • COOKING TIME: 10 minutes

INGREDIENTS

¾ cup (180 ml) pineapple or orange juice

¼ cup (60 ml) nonfat powdered milk

¼ tsp ground cardamom

½ cup (125 ml) whole wheat couscous

¼ cup (60 ml) dried cranberries, chopped

For the caramelized almonds

2 tsp water

2 tsp brown sugar

½ cup (125 ml) almonds

METHOD

In a small saucepan over high heat, bring fruit juice to a boil. Gradually add milk and cardamom. Remove from heat and add couscous. Cover and let rest for 5 minutes. Add cranberries and mix well.

In a small skillet over medium heat, combine water, brown sugar and almonds. Cook for 7 minutes or until almonds have caramelized. (The liquid will be absorbed after 5 minutes and the almonds will turn golden brown 1 or 2 minutes after that.)

Serve couscous topped with caramelized almonds.

• • • • • • • • • • • • • •

TIP

Prepare a batch of caramelized almonds and serve with yogurt, ice cream, fruit or vegetable salads, etc.

SPORTS INFO

It is recommended that you decrease your consumption of whole-grain products 2 or 3 days prior to a major sporting event in order to prevent gastrointestinal discomfort. In this case, regular couscous can be replaced with whole wheat couscous.

Nutrition Facts Per serving	
Amount	
Calories	579 kcal
Fat	21 g
Sodium	78 mg
Carbohydrate	84 g
Fiber	8 g
Protein	19 g

GRANOLA
#2

13 servings • PREPARATION: 10 minutes • COOKING TIME: 25 minutes

INGREDIENTS

1½ cups (375 ml) old-fashioned rolled oats (not instant)

1½ cups (375 ml) rye flakes

1 cup (250 ml) pecans

½ cup (125 ml) shredded unsweetened coconut

½ cup (125 ml) pumpkin seeds

¼ cup (60 ml) butter, melted

½ cup (125 ml) honey

½ cup (125 ml) dried cranberries

METHOD

Position rack in middle of oven and preheat to 300°F (150°C). Line a baking sheet with parchment paper.

In a bowl, combine all ingredients except cranberries. Spread over prepared baking sheet and cook in middle of preheated oven, for 25 minutes, stirring halfway through cooking.

Add cranberries and stir.

• • • • • • • • • • • • • •

VARIATIONS

- You can replace the pumpkin seeds with other seeds (e.g. sunflower seeds) and the pecans with other nuts (e.g. walnuts, pistachios).

- You can also replace the butter with coconut oil.

• • • • • • • • • • • • • •

TIPS

- The granola can be stored in an airtight container at room temperature for 6 months.

- The granola can be eaten in various ways. Have it plain to satisfy a small craving; stir it into yogurt, milk or soy milk; or sprinkle it over applesauce, fruit salad, ice cream or sorbet.

Nutrition Facts
Per ½ cup (125 ml)

Amount	
Calories	249 kcal
Fat	13 g
Sodium	4 mg
Carbohydrate	32 g
Fiber	4 g
Protein	5 g

Drink

1 serving • PREPARATION: 5 minutes

INGREDIENTS

5 oz (150 g) coconut-flavored silken tofu

½ cup (125 ml) Greek yogurt, plain

1 banana

½ cup (125 ml) diced fresh or frozen pineapple

1 tbsp chia seeds (optional)

METHOD

Place all ingredients in a blender and mix until smooth.

Pour beverage into a glass or an airtight container.

• • • • • • • • • • • • • •

TIP

Prepare this breakfast the day before and refrigerate it overnight. Store it in your workout bag next to a freezer pack (e.g. reusable ice pack) or in a thermos to keep it cool until you're ready to drink.

SPORTS INFO

A breakfast drink is a practical option for your morning workouts. That way, you don't have to wait to get home or to work to eat. To maximize recovery, you should eat within 30 minutes of completing your workout.

Nutrition Facts
Per serving

Amount	
Calories	376 kcal
Fat	6 g
Sodium	59 mg
Carbohydrate	63 g
Fiber	8 g
Protein	21 g

ENERGY
Balls

25 balls • PREPARATION: 15 minutes • COOKING TIME: 10 minutes

METHOD

In a small saucepan over medium-high heat, cook dates in water for 10 minutes or until they become soft.

Using a hand blender, purée dates with cooking water. Add cocoa powder and stir using a wooden spoon. Add peanut butter and mix until smooth. Add graham cracker crumbs and stir again.

Using your hands, roll mixture into 25 balls measuring about 1½ inches (4 cm) in diameter. Eat right away or refrigerate in an airtight container.

• • • • • • • • • • • • •

VARIATION

You can substitute the graham cracker crumbs with the same amount of rolled oats.

• • • • • • • • • • • • •

TIP

The balls can be stored in an airtight bag in the freezer for up to 3 months. They can be eaten just minutes after being removed from the freezer.

INGREDIENTS

2 cups (500 ml) pitted dates

1 cup (250 ml) water

¼ cup (60 ml) cocoa powder

¾ cup (180 ml) peanut butter

3 cups (750 ml) graham cracker crumbs

Nutrition Facts
Per ball

Amount	
Calories	138 kcal
Fat	5 g
Sodium	66 mg
Carbohydrate	22 g
Fiber	2 g
Protein	3 g

CHOCOLATE
Pudding

4 servings • PREPARATION: 10 minutes • COOKING TIME: 15 minutes • REFRIGERATION: 2 hours

INGREDIENTS

2 oz (60 g) unsweetened baking chocolate, coarsely chopped

2 tbsp cocoa powder

¼ cup (60 ml) cornstarch

½ cup (125 ml) nonfat powdered milk

¼ cup (60 ml) granulated sugar

¼ tsp ground cinnamon

2½ cups (625 ml) 1% milk

2 tsp vanilla extract

METHOD

Melt chocolate in a double boiler over high heat. Set aside.

In a heavy-bottomed saucepan, combine cocoa, cornstarch, powdered milk, sugar and cinnamon. Add milk, then melted chocolate and whisk.

Bring mixture to a boil over medium-high heat, whisking occasionally. Cook for 2 minutes, scraping bottom of saucepan continuously with a silicone spatula until mixture becomes thick and shiny. Add vanilla.

Pour mixture into containers, cover and refrigerate for at least 2 hours.

• • • • • • • • • • • •

TIP

This pudding can be stored in airtight containers for up to 5 days.

SPORTS INFO

This recipe is a good source of protein (to repair muscle fibers) and carbohydrates (to replenish glycogen reserves). To optimize recovery, it is recommended that you eat within 30 minutes of exercising.

Nutrition Facts Per serving	
Amount	
Calories	282 kcal
Fat	10 g
Sodium	143 mg
Carbohydrate	41 g
Fiber	3 g
Protein	12 g

PINEAPPLE STRAWBERRY
Salad

6 servings • PREPARATION: 15 minutes

INGREDIENTS

1 pineapple, cut into chunks

3 cups (750 ml) strawberries, sliced

Zest and juice of 1 lime

METHOD

In a bowl, combine all ingredients.

• • • • • • • • • • • • •

TIPS

- The fruit salad can be stored in an airtight container in the refrigerator for up to 5 days.
- Lime zest and juice add a touch of freshness to any fruit salad.

Nutrition Facts	
Per serving	
Amount	
Calories	64 kcal
Fat	0 g
Sodium	2 mg
Carbohydrate	16 g
Fiber	3 g
Protein	1 g

BLUEBERRY HAZELNUT
Muffins

12 muffins • PREPARATION: 15 minutes • COOKING TIME: 25 minutes

INGREDIENTS

¾ cup (180 ml) quick-cooking rolled oats

¾ cup (180 ml) all-purpose flour

2 tsp baking powder

1 tsp baking soda

½ tsp salt

¾ cup (180 ml) brown sugar

¾ cup (180 ml) ground hazelnuts

2 eggs

¼ cup (60 ml) canola oil

1 cup (250 ml) Greek yogurt, plain

1 tsp vanilla extract

Zest of 1 lemon

1 cup (250 ml) frozen blueberries

METHOD

Position rack in middle of oven and preheat to 375°F (190°C). Line a 12-cup muffin tin with paper or silicone liners.

In a large bowl, combine rolled oats, flour, baking powder, baking soda, salt, brown sugar and hazelnuts.

In a separate bowl, whisk eggs, oil, yogurt, vanilla and lemon zest. Pour into bowl with flour mixture. Using a spatula, stir until dry ingredients are slightly moistened. Add blueberries and fold evenly into the batter.

Pour mixture into prepared muffin cups and cook in middle of oven for 25 minutes or until a toothpick inserted in center of a muffin comes out clean. Allow muffins to cool before unmolding.

• • • • • • • • • • • • • •

TIP

The muffins can be stored in an airtight container at room temperature for up to 3 days. You can also freeze them in an airtight bag for up to 3 months.

Nutrition Facts	
Per muffin	
Amount	
Calories	249 kcal
Fat	14 g
Sodium	195 mg
Carbohydrate	25 g
Fiber	2 g
Protein	6 g

CHEWS

25 chews • PREPARATION: 10 minutes • COOKING TIME: 5 minutes
REFRIGERATION: 4 hours • RESTING TIME: 4 hours

INGREDIENTS

4 envelopes (each ¼ oz/7 g) gelatin

2 cups (500 ml) orange juice

1½ cups (375 ml) granulated sugar

2 tbsp lemon juice

SPORTS INFO

• •

To maintain a constant energy level throughout long workouts or races, it is recommended that you eat at least 30 g of carbohydrates per hour (up to 90 g for an ultramarathon). Refer to the nutrition info table provided for these chews.

Nutrition Facts Per chew	
Amount	
Calories	60 kcal
Fat	0 g
Sodium	2 mg
Carbohydrate	14 g
Fiber	0 g
Protein	1 g

METHOD

Line a 9-inch (23 cm) square pan with a sheet of lightly greased plastic wrap.

Place orange juice in a saucepan and sprinkle with gelatin (do not stir). Let soak for several minutes. Add sugar and lemon juice. Warm mixture over medium heat for 5 minutes until gelatin and sugar have completely dissolved.

Pour mixture into prepared pan. Refrigerate for at least 4 hours.

Once mixture has set, unmold and cut into 25 equal pieces. Let rest on a paper towel at room temperature for about 4 hours before eating. Refrigerate chews in an airtight container (see Tip).

• • • • • • • • • • • • •

VARIATION

You can use the fruit juice of your choice and even incorporate fruit purée. Keep in mind that certain fruits (and their freshly squeezed juice) contain enzymes that prevent gelatin from setting (especially pineapple, papaya, kiwi, guava and honeydew melon). If you wish to use freshly squeezed juice from those fruits, boil the juice first to deactivate the enzymes or use pasteurized juice.

• • • • • • • • • • • • •

TIP

The chews can be stored in an airtight container in the refrigerator for up to 7 days. Do not freeze them.

Smoothies

3 servings • PREPARATION: 5 minutes

METHOD

Place all ingredients in a blender and mix until smooth.

• • • • • • • • • • • • • •

TIP

Divide smoothie into three airtight containers (each 2 cups/500 ml). These can be kept in the refrigerator for 1 or 2 days or in the freezer for up to 3 months.

INGREDIENTS

¾ cup (180 ml) Greek yogurt, plain

1 cup (250 ml) 1% milk

1 cup (250 ml) pineapple juice

1 banana

1 cup (250 ml) frozen peaches

SPORTS INFO

• •

After intense exercise lasting 60 to 90 minutes, a snack that delivers 30 to 45 g of carbohydrates and about 10 g of proteins is sufficient to promote recovery. This smoothie is also effective for rehydrating since it is a beverage.

Nutrition Facts
Per serving

Amount	
Calories	195 kcal
Fat	1 g
Sodium	65 mg
Carbohydrate	38 g
Fiber	2 g
Protein	10 g

CHEWY
Bars

20 bars • PREPARATION: 10 minutes • COOKING TIME: 25 minutes

INGREDIENTS

1 can (14 oz or 300 ml) sweetened condensed milk

1 egg, beaten

1 tsp vanilla extract

3 cups (750 ml) quick-cooking rolled oats

¾ cup (180 ml) dried cranberries

¾ cup (180 ml) slivered almonds, toasted

¾ cup (180 ml) shredded unsweetened coconut

¾ cup (180 ml) chocolate chips

¼ cup (60 ml) flaxseeds (optional)

METHOD

Position rack in middle of oven and preheat to 350°F (180°C). Grease a 9-inch (23 cm) square pan.

In a bowl, combine condensed milk, egg and vanilla.

In a large bowl, mix rolled oats, cranberries, almonds, coconut, chocolate chips and flaxseeds. Add liquid mixture and mix well.

Pour the mixture into prepared pan. Cook in middle of oven for 20 to 25 minutes. Allow to cool before unmolding. Cut into 20 bars.

• • • • • • • • • • • • • •

VARIATION

You can replace the cranberries with other dried fruit, the almonds with other nuts, and the coconut with seeds.

• • • • • • • • • • • • • •

TIP

The bars can be stored in an airtight container at room temperature for up to 7 days or in the freezer for up to 3 months.

Nutrition Facts	
Per bar	
Amount	
Calories	224 kcal
Fat	10 g
Sodium	34 mg
Carbohydrate	30 g
Fiber	3 g
Protein	5 g

SWEET RICE
Balls

24 balls • PREPARATION: 10 minutes • COOKING TIME: 20 minutes

INGREDIENTS

1½ cups (375 ml) water

1 cup (250 ml) risotto or sushi rice

¼ cup (60 ml) sesame seeds

¼ cup (60 ml) shredded unsweetened coconut

2 tbsp honey

½ tsp vanilla extract

Nutrition Facts
For 3 balls

Amount	
Calories	158 kcal
Fat	4 g
Sodium	2 mg
Carbohydrate	27 g
Fiber	2 g
Protein	3 g

METHOD

Bring water to a boil in a saucepan over high heat. Add rice and stir. Cover and cook over low heat for 15 to 20 minutes according to package directions. Allow to cool.

Meanwhile, in a nonstick skillet over medium-high heat, toast sesame seeds and coconut until lightly browned. Set aside in a bowl.

In a separate bowl, combine rice, honey and vanilla. Using your hands, shape 24 balls (about 2 tbsp of mixture per ball).

Roll balls in sesame seeds and coconut.

• • • • • • • • • • • • •

VARIATIONS

You can add the following to the plain rice, once it has cooled:

- ⅓ cup (80 ml) raisins + 2 tbsp brown sugar + 1 tsp ground cinnamon + ¼ tsp ground nutmeg
- ¼ cup (60 ml) chocolate chips + 1 tbsp white or brown sugar + ½ tsp cayenne pepper

• • • • • • • • • • • • •

TIP

The rice balls can be stored in an airtight container for up to 6 days in the refrigerator or up to 6 months in the freezer.

BROWNIE
in a Cup

1 serving • PREPARATION: 5 minutes • COOKING TIME: 1 minute

INGREDIENTS

1 tbsp all-purpose flour

2 tbsp powdered milk

2 tbsp granulated sugar

1 tbsp cocoa powder

2 tbsp 1% milk

METHOD

In a bowl, combine all ingredients.

Pour mixture into a microwave-safe cup and microwave on High (1200 watts) for 1 minute.

• • • • • • • • • • • • •

TIP

If your microwave is more powerful (e.g. 1500 watts), set power at 80% and use the same cooking time (1 minute).

Nutrition Facts
Per serving

Amount	
Calories	210 kcal
Fat	2 g
Sodium	95 mg
Carbohydrate	44 g
Fiber	2 g
Protein	8 g

GREEN
Smoothie

1 serving • PREPARATION: 5 minutes

INGREDIENTS

1 cup (250 ml) unsweetened almond milk

1 kiwi, peeled and cut into pieces

1 leaf kale, torn into pieces
(stem removed)

1 tbsp oat bran

METHOD

Place all ingredients in a blender and blend until smooth.

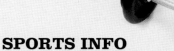

SPORTS INFO

• •

If you plan on working out as soon as you jump out of bed, it is a good idea to eat or drink something light before exercising. This green smoothie is the perfect solution, since it is hydrating and contains carbohydrates to give you energy.

Nutrition Facts Per serving	
Amount	
Calories	100 kcal
Fat	3 g
Sodium	160 mg
Carbohydrate	18 g
Fiber	4 g
Protein	3 g

TORTILLA
Chips

2 servings • PREPARATION: 5 minutes • COOKING TIME: 15 minutes

METHOD

Position rack in bottom of oven and preheat to 350°F (180°C). Line two baking sheets with parchment paper.

In a bowl, combine oil, oregano and chili seasoning.

Using a brush, apply oil mixture to each side of tortillas. Cut each tortilla into 8 wedges and arrange wedges on prepared baking sheets. Position baking sheets one at a time in bottom of oven and cook for 7 to 8 minutes or until chips are crunchy.

• • • • • • • • • • • • •

VARIATION

Replace suggested seasoning with fresh crushed garlic, smoked paprika or any spice of your choice.

• • • • • • • • • • • • •

TIP

The chips can be stored in an airtight container at room temperature for 7 days. Make sure they are cool before placing them in container.

INGREDIENTS

1 tsp canola oil

½ tsp dried oregano

1 tsp chili seasoning

4 6-inch (15 cm) whole wheat tortillas

Nutrition Facts Per serving	
Amount	
Calories	233 kcal
Fat	7 g
Sodium	319 mg
Carbohydrate	36 g
Fiber	3 g
Protein	6 g

RED
Smoothie

1 serving • PREPARATION: 5 minutes

INGREDIENTS

1 cup (250 ml) almond milk

½ cup (125 ml) grape juice

½ cup (125 ml) frozen strawberries

¼ cup (60 ml) whey powder

METHOD

Place all ingredients in a blender and mix until smooth.

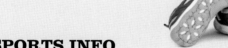

SPORTS INFO

••

If you are an athlete and train intensely almost every day, or even several times a day, it is essential that you recover between intense workouts. Full of carbohydrates, proteins and water, this smoothie delivers the raw material you need to replenish depleted energy reserves.

Nutrition Facts Per serving	
Amount	
Calories	253 kcal
Fat	3 g
Sodium	321 mg
Carbohydrate	31 g
Fiber	1 g
Protein	27 g

SAVORY
Rice Balls

24 balls • PREPARATION: 15 minutes • COOKING TIME: 20 minutes

INGREDIENTS

1½ cups (375 ml) water

1 cup (250 ml) risotto or sushi rice

1 tsp salt

1 tsp ground cumin

1 tsp chili seasoning

½ can (19 oz/540 ml) black beans, drained and rinsed

½ cup (125 ml) grated sharp cheddar

Black pepper

Nutrition Facts For 3 balls	
Amount	
Calories	152 kcal
Fat	3 g
Sodium	409 mg
Carbohydrate	26 g
Fiber	2 g
Protein	5 g

METHOD

Bring water to a boil in a saucepan over high heat. Add rice and salt. Cover and cook over low heat for 15 to 20 minutes according to package directions. Allow to cool.

Meanwhile, in a nonstick skillet over medium-high heat, heat cumin and chili seasoning for 30 seconds.

In a bowl, combine rice, spices, beans and cheese. Season with pepper.

Loosely cover an ice cube tray with a sheet of plastic wrap. Drop 1 tbsp of mixture into each cube (about 24 cubes) and press down firmly. To remove the balls, simply lift the plastic wrap out of the ice cube tray.

• • • • • • • • • • • • •

VARIATION

You can substitute the black beans, cumin and chili seasoning with 3 strips (3 oz/90 g) of cooked and chopped bacon.

• • • • • • • • • • • • •

TIPS

• This quantity of canned beans yields about 2 cups (500 ml) cooked. If you want to start with dried beans, use 1 cup (250 ml) and soak and cook.

• You can also roll a dozen balls by hand or simply eat the rice with a fork. It is delicious served warm or cold.

• The rice balls can be stored in an airtight container in the refrigerator for up to 6 days or in the freezer for up to 6 months.

CHICKEN
Pizza

4 servings • PREPARATION: 40 minutes • COOKING TIME: 20 minutes

INGREDIENTS

2 cups (500 ml) all-purpose flour, divided

1 envelope (¼ oz/8 g) pizza crust yeast

1½ tsp granulated sugar

¼ tsp salt

⅔ cup (160 ml) water, as hot as possible from the tap

3 tbsp olive oil

For the topping

1 tsp olive oil

⅔ lb (325 g) boneless skinless chicken breast, cut into strips

1 cup (250 ml) acorn squash purée

2 cups (500 ml) arugula

½ onion, chopped

4 oz (125 g) mozzarella, sliced

Nutrition Facts	
Per serving	
Amount	
Calories	586 kcal
Fat	15 g
Sodium	574 mg
Carbohydrate	63 g
Fiber	4 g
Protein	32 g

METHOD

Place a baking sheet on a rack in bottom of oven and preheat to 400°F (200°C). Line another baking sheet with parchment paper.

In a bowl, combine 1 cup (250 ml) flour, yeast, sugar and salt.

In a measuring cup, combine water and oil. Pour into bowl with flour mixture. Using a wooden spoon, stir for 1 minute until mixture is almost smooth. Add as much of remaining flour as possible and stir until a ball of dough forms.

On a floured work surface, knead dough for several minutes until it is no longer sticky. Using your hands or a rolling pin, stretch out dough on prepared baking sheet. Cover with a sheet of plastic wrap and set aside.

Heat oil in a nonstick skillet over high heat and brown chicken strips for 2 minutes on each side.

Meanwhile, spread squash purée over pizza dough. Top with arugula, chicken, onion and finally mozzarella. Remove baking sheet from oven. Slide pizza and parchment paper onto warmed baking sheet. Cook in bottom of oven for 15 minutes or until crust turns golden brown.

• • • • • • • • • • • • • •

VARIATION

Use flat bread if you don't want to make your own pizza dough.

CRISPY TOFU
with Broccoli

3 servings • PREPARATION: 15 minutes • COOKING TIME: 20 minutes

INGREDIENTS

1 block (16 oz/454 g) firm tofu, cut into ¾-inch (2 cm) cubes

2 tbsp cornstarch

½ to 1 cup (125 to 250 ml) canola oil

For the sauce

¼ cup (60 ml) low-sodium soy sauce

3 tbsp maple syrup

1 tsp Sriracha sauce

For the Broccoli

2 cups (500 ml) broccoli florets

1 clove garlic, chopped

2 tsp canola oil

1 tsp oyster sauce

1 tbsp water

METHOD

Place tofu in a bowl and sprinkle with cornstarch. Stir gently until all cubes are well coated.

In a skillet, heat oil over medium-high heat. Add tofu cubes, spacing them as much as possible. Cook for 3 to 4 minutes. Turn over and cook for 3 to 4 more minutes. Repeat until every side is golden brown.

Remove excess oil, then add sauce ingredients. Bring to a boil, stirring to coat tofu with sauce.

Meanwhile, in a large skillet over medium-high heat, sauté broccoli and garlic in oil for 1 minute. Add oyster sauce and water. Continue cooking for 1 minute.

Serve tofu with broccoli on the side.

Nutrition Facts Per serving	
Amount	
Calories	345 kcal
Fat	27 g
Sodium	657 mg
Carbohydrate	27 g
Fiber	2 g
Protein	24 g

HERRING
alla Puttanesca

1 serving • PREPARATION: 15 minutes • COOKING TIME: 15 minutes

METHOD

In a saucepan, cook pasta according to package directions until al dente. Drain, reserving ¼ cup (60 ml) of pasta water.

Meanwhile, heat oil in a skillet over medium-high heat and sauté onion until translucent. Add tomatoes and continue cooking for 2 to 3 minutes.

Add olives, capers and parsley and stir. Cook for 2 to 3 minutes. Add herring and stir gently. Pour in reserved pasta water and reduce for 1 to 2 minutes. Add pasta, mix and season with pepper.

• • • • • • • • • • • • •

TIP

Canned herring is an eco-friendly, nutritious and practical choice. Keep several cans in your cupboard so you always have a quick source of protein on hand.

INGREDIENTS

3 oz (90 g) capellini

2 tsp olive oil

1 onion, diced

2 plum (Roma) tomatoes, diced

¼ cup (60 ml) Kalamata olives, pitted

1 tsp capers

1 tbsp chopped fresh parsley

1 can (3 oz/92 g) herring (in tomato sauce or in lemon and cracked pepper)

Black pepper

Nutrition Facts
Per serving

Amount	
Calories	680 kcal
Fat	22 g
Sodium	532 mg
Carbohydrate	90 g
Fiber	6 g
Protein	33 g

QUICK COUSCOUS
with Black Beans and Vegetables

1 serving • PREPARATION: 5 minutes • COOKING TIME: 3 minutes

INGREDIENTS

⅓ cup (80 ml) uncooked couscous

1 cup (250 ml) frozen diced mixed vegetables

1 tsp harissa

⅓ cup (80 ml) chicken broth

⅓ cup (80 ml) water

¾ cup (180 ml) canned black beans, drained and rinsed

METHOD

In the microwave

In a large microwave-safe cup, combine couscous, vegetables, harissa, chicken broth and water. Microwave on High (1200 watts) for 3 minutes. Add black beans and stir.

On the stovetop

In a saucepan over medium-high heat, bring broth and water to a boil. Add couscous while stirring, then add vegetables and harissa. Cook over low heat, stirring occasionally, for 1 to 2 minutes, until couscous expands and all the broth has been absorbed. Add beans and stir.

SPORTS INFO

• •

This couscous dish is an excellent post-workout meal when you come home ravenous. It is easy to prepare and very satisfying.

Nutrition Facts Per serving	
Amount	
Calories	526 kcal
Fat	2 g
Sodium	625 mg
Carbohydrate	102 g
Fiber	20 g
Protein	27 g

BEET
Patties

4 patties • PREPARATION: 15 minutes • RESTING TIME: 15 minutes • COOKING TIME: 10 minutes

INGREDIENTS

2 beets, peeled and grated

1 egg

¾ cup (180 ml) quick-cooking rolled oats

⅔ cup (160 ml) crumbled goat cheese

1 tsp olive oil

1 clove garlic, chopped

1 tbsp chopped fresh basil

1 tbsp chopped fresh mint leaves

Pinch salt

½ tsp ground black pepper

2 tbsp canola oil

METHOD

In a large bowl, combine all ingredients except for canola oil. Let rest for 15 minutes.

Using your hands, form 4 patties measuring about 4 inches (10 cm) in diameter.

In a large nonstick skillet over medium-high heat, heat canola oil and cook patties for 4 to 5 minutes. Flip patties with a spatula and continue cooking for 4 to 5 minutes.

• • • • • • • • • • • • • •

TIPS

- Serve patties with Edamame Purée (p. 152) on the side or as a topping.
- The patties can be frozen after cooking.

Nutrition Facts 2 patties	
Amount	
Calories	416 kcal
Fat	24 g
Sodium	424 mg
Carbohydrate	30 g
Fiber	5 g
Protein	20 g

EDAMAME
Purée

2 servings • PREPARATION: 5 minutes

INGREDIENTS

1 cup (250 ml) frozen edamame

2 cups (500 ml) arugula

2 tbsp tahini (sesame butter)

2 tbsp water

1 tbsp balsamic vinegar

1 tbsp lemon juice

¼ tsp salt

¼ tsp black pepper

Nutrition Facts
Per serving

Amount	
Calories	190 kcal
Fat	12 g
Sodium	266 mg
Carbohydrate	13 g
Fiber	5 g
Protein	10 g

METHOD
In the microwave

In a microwave-safe bowl, cook edamame on High (1200 watts) in ¼ cup (60 ml) of water for 3 to 4 minutes.

Purée all ingredients in a food processor.

On the stovetop

Pour ½ cup (125 ml) water in a small saucepan over high heat. Place a vegetable steamer (or metal colander) over saucepan. Once water starts to boil, place edamame in vegetable steamer. Cook for 4 to 5 minutes. Run edamame under cold water to cool.

Purée all ingredients in a food processor.

• • • • • • • • • • • • •

TIPS

- You can use the edamame purée as a topping for veggie burgers (see Beet Patties, p. 150).

- The edamame purée can be stored in an airtight container in the refrigerator for up to 4 days.

CHICKEN DRUMSTICKS
with Polenta

4 servings • PREPARATION: 40 minutes • COOKING TIME: 45 minutes

INGREDIENTS

3 tbsp Dijon mustard

1 tsp smoked paprika

½ tsp dried oregano

¼ tsp salt

8 chicken drumsticks

For the Polenta

2½ cups (625 ml) water

⅔ cup (160 ml) cornmeal

2 tbsp butter

⅓ cup (80 ml) grated Parmesan cheese

Salt and pepper

METHOD

Position rack in middle of oven and preheat to 425°F (220°C). Line a baking sheet with parchment paper.

In a bowl, mix mustard, paprika, oregano and salt. On prepared baking sheet coat chicken drumsticks with mustard mixture. Cook in middle of preheated oven for 45 minutes or until internal temperature reaches 165°F (74°C), turning drumsticks every 15 minutes.

Meanwhile, in a heavy-bottomed saucepan over high heat, bring water to a boil. Add cornmeal, whisking constantly until mixture begins to thicken. Continue cooking at medium-low heat, stirring occasionally, for 25 to 30 minutes. Add butter and Parmesan cheese. Season to taste.

Serve drumsticks with polenta.

Nutrition Facts Per serving	
Amount	
Calories	393 kcal
Fat	24 g
Sodium	501 mg
Carbohydrate	17 g
Fiber	2 g
Protein	28 g

WHITE BEAN
and Sautéed Vegetable Wraps

3 servings • PREPARATION: 15 minutes • COOKING TIME: 5 minutes

METHOD

In a food processor, combine ingredients for the filling and purée.

Heat oil in a large nonstick skillet over medium-high heat. Sauté onion, bell pepper, cumin, salt and pepper for 4 to 5 minutes or until vegetables are tender. Add cilantro and stir.

Spread bean mixture over tortillas and top with sautéed vegetables. Roll up tortillas.

• • • • • • • • • • • • •

TIP

This quantity of canned beans yields about 2 cups (500 mL) cooked. If you want to start with dried beans, use 1 cup (250 mL) and soak and cook.

INGREDIENTS

2 tsp olive oil
1 yellow onion, thinly sliced
1 red bell pepper, thinly sliced
¼ tsp ground cumin
Pinch salt
¼ tsp black pepper
2 tbsp chopped fresh cilantro
3 9-inch (23 cm) whole wheat tortillas

For the filling

1 can (19 oz/540 ml) white beans, drained and rinsed (see Tip)
2 tbsp lemon juice
2 or 3 tbsp water (depending on desired consistency)
¼ tsp salt
¼ tsp black pepper

Nutrition Facts
Per serving

Amount

Calories	558 kcal
Fat	19 g
Sodium	464 mg
Carbohydrate	79 g
Fiber	13 g
Protein	19 g

HONEY MUSTARD
Arctic Char

2 servings • PREPARATION: 10 minutes • COOKING TIME: 10 minutes

INGREDIENTS

1 Artic char fillet (½ lb/250 g)

1 tbsp Dijon mustard

1 tbsp honey

¼ onion, chopped

1 tsp fennel seeds

For the fennel salad

2 tsp olive oil

1 tsp balsamic vinegar

2 cups (500 ml) thinly sliced fennel

1 tsp salt

Black pepper

METHOD

Position rack in bottom of oven and pre-heat to 450°F (225°C).

Place Arctic char in center of a large sheet of aluminum foil. Fold up sides of foil around fish leaving the fish exposed on the top. Place on a baking sheet.

In a small bowl, combine mustard, honey, onion and fennel seeds. Use a spoon to pour mixture over fish. Cook in bottom of oven for 10 minutes.

Meanwhile, in a separate bowl, combine oil, vinegar and fennel. Season with salt and pepper.

Serve fillet with fennel salad.

• • • • • • • • • • • • •

TIP

If you only eat one serving of the fish, you can keep the remainder for the next day to make a sandwich or salad (see Farfalle Salad with Arctic Char, p. 164).

Nutrition Facts Per serving	
Amount	
Calories	227 kcal
Fat	6 g
Sodium	464 mg
Carbohydrate	18 g
Fiber	3 g
Protein	26 g

HEARTY
Legume Soup

8 servings • PREPARATION: 15 minutes • COOKING TIME: 35 minutes

INGREDIENTS

2 tbsp olive oil

2 cloves garlic, crushed

3 carrots, diced

3 stalks celery, diced

2 cups (500 ml) chopped green cabbage

2 tbsp grated fresh ginger

8 cups (2 l) chicken broth

2 bay leaves

1 can (14 oz/398 ml) diced seasoned tomatoes

2 cans (each 19 oz/540 ml) black-eyed peas, drained and rinsed

1 block (16 oz/454 g) extra firm tofu, diced

½ cup (125 ml) quinoa, uncooked

1 tbsp Italian seasoning

Salt and freshly ground pepper

METHOD

Heat oil in a large saucepan over medium-high heat. Sauté garlic, carrots, celery, cabbage and ginger for 5 minutes or until vegetables are tender.

Add broth and bay leaves, then bring to a boil. Reduce heat to medium-low. Cover and let simmer for about 20 minutes.

Add tomatoes, peas, tofu, quinoa and Italian seasoning. Cover and continue cooking for about 10 minutes. Season with salt and freshly ground pepper.

SPORTS INFO

If you aren't used to eating legumes, you may initially experience some discomfort (e.g. bloating or gas). Don't worry, your digestive system will become accustomed to legumes over time. However, to avoid any discomfort during an important workout or sporting event, refrain from eating legumes the day before and the day of your workout or sporting event.

Nutrition Facts For 2 cups (500 ml)	
Amount	
Calories	289 kcal
Fat	9 g
Sodium	656 mg
Carbohydrate	40 g
Fiber	9 g
Protein	22 g

PAN-FRIED WHITE BEANS
with Creamed Spinach

2 servings • PREPARATION: 10 minutes • COOKING TIME: 15 minutes

INGREDIENTS

4 tsp butter

2 slices (2 oz/60 g) bacon, cut into strips

1 can (19 oz/540 ml) white beans, drained and rinsed (see Tip)

1 cup (250 ml) diced leeks

2 cloves garlic, chopped

1 tbsp white wine vinegar

For the Creamed Spinach

2 tsp butter

1 clove garlic, chopped

6 cups (1.5 l) spinach

3 tbsp table (18%) cream

Salt and pepper

METHOD

In a large nonstick skillet over medium heat, melt butter. Add bacon and beans. Cook without stirring for 3 to 4 minutes. Mix well and continue cooking for 3 to 4 minutes. Add leeks and garlic and cook for 2 minutes until leeks become tender. Add vinegar. Season with pepper and mix.

Meanwhile, in a skillet over medium-high heat, melt butter. Add garlic and spinach. Cover and cook for 2 minutes. Add cream. Reduce for 2 minutes. Season with salt and pepper.

Serve beans with creamed spinach.

• • • • • • • • • • • • • •

TIP

This quantity of canned beans yields about 2 cups (500 mL) cooked. If you want to start with dried beans, use 1 cup (250 mL) and soak and cook.

Nutrition Facts
Per serving

Amount	
Calories	619 kcal
Fat	30 g
Sodium	596 mg
Carbohydrate	64 g
Fiber	17 g
Protein	28 g

FARFALLE SALAD
with Arctic Char

1 serving • PREPARATION: 10 minutes • COOKING TIME: 15 minutes

INGREDIENTS

1½ cups (375 ml) farfalle

1 tbsp olive oil

2 tsp balsamic vinegar

Black pepper

¾ cup (180 ml) cooked Arctic char, flaked (about 3½ oz/100 g)

6 Kalamata olives, chopped

½ red bell pepper, diced

1 cup (250 ml) arugula

METHOD

In a large saucepan, cook pasta according to package directions. Drain.

Meanwhile, in a bowl, combine oil and vinegar. Season with pepper.

Pour vinaigrette over warm pasta. Add Arctic char, olives, bell pepper and arugula. Mix well.

• • • • • • • • • • • • •

TIP

This salad is delicious served warm or cold. You can transport it in an airtight container and eat it immediately after working out, wherever you are.

Nutrition Facts
Per serving

Amount	
Calories	625 kcal
Fat	22 g
Sodium	349 mg
Carbohydrate	67 g
Fiber	4 g
Protein	38 g

PORK AND MINT
Vermicelli

3 servings • PREPARATION: 10 minutes • COOKING TIME: 10 minutes

METHOD

Heat oil in a large nonstick skillet over high heat. Sauté pork for 4 to 5 minutes on each side until golden brown. Add garlic and stir.

Meanwhile, place vermicelli in a large bowl and cover with boiling water. Let soak for 5 minutes, then drain.

In a separate bowl, combine pork, green onion, fish sauce, lime juice, brown sugar, sambal oelek and mint.

In a microwave-safe bowl, cook vegetables on High (1200 watts) for 3 minutes.

To serve, arrange vermicelli, meat and vegetables in bowls. Spoon sauce over vermicelli and garnish with peanuts.

INGREDIENTS

1 tbsp canola oil

1 10 oz (300 g) pork tenderloin, cut into strips or chopped

2 cloves garlic, chopped

7 oz (210 g) soy vermicelli

1 green onion, sliced

4 tsp fish sauce (e.g. nuoc mam)

3 tbsp lime juice

½ tsp brown sugar

1 tsp sambal oelek

¼ cup (60 ml) fresh mint leaves, coarsely chopped

1½ cups (375 ml) frozen Asian vegetables

¼ cup (60 ml) peanuts, coarsely chopped

Nutrition Facts
Per serving

Amount	
Calories	593 kcal
Fat	19 g
Sodium	349 mg
Carbohydrate	76 g
Fiber	8 g
Protein	32 g

OMELET
in a Cup

1 serving • PREPARATION: 5 minutes • COOKING TIME: 4 minutes

INGREDIENTS

3 eggs, beaten

3 tbsp 1% milk

½ tsp low-sodium soy sauce

¼ tsp Tabasco sauce

1 tbsp chopped fresh dill

¼ cup (60 ml) grated Gruyère cheese

METHOD

In a bowl, whisk eggs, milk, soy sauce, Tabasco sauce and dill. Pour in a micro-wave-safe cup and sprinkle with cheese. Microwave on Medium (600 watts) for 4 minutes.

• • • • • • • • • • • • •

TIP

If you're looking for something easy to serve with this omelet, you can use frozen mixed vegetables. Heat vegetables in a microwave-safe bowl on High (1200 watts) for 1 to 2 minutes. Drain and season with salt and pepper.

Nutrition Facts
Per serving

Amount	
Calories	298 kcal
Fat	21 g
Sodium	349 mg
Carbohydrate	4 g
Fiber	0 g
Protein	23 g

CHICKEN
Fried Rice

2 servings • PREPARATION: 10 minutes • COOKING TIME: 10 minutes

INGREDIENTS

1 tbsp canola oil

1 clove garlic, crushed

2 carrots, peeled and sliced

½ lb (250 g) skinless boneless chicken breast, cut into ½-inch (1 cm) cubes

3 eggs

2 cups (500 ml) cooked brown rice (see Tip)

4 tsp low-sodium soy sauce

1 tsp fish sauce (e.g. nuoc mam)

½ tsp Sriracha sauce

2 tbsp lime juice

1 seedless cucumber, sliced

1 tomato, quartered

1 green onion, sliced

METHOD

In a large nonstick skillet over medium-high heat, brown garlic in oil. Add carrots and chicken and cook until chicken has browned. Push mixture to edge of skillet. Crack eggs into skillet and stir with a wooden spoon for 1 minute.

Mix together chicken, carrots and eggs. Add rice and sauces. Stir again and continue cooking until a sizzling sound is heard and rice begins to look dry. Add lime juice and stir.

Serve with cucumber, tomato and green onion.

• • • • • • • • • • • • • •

TIP

Use ⅔ cup (160 ml) uncooked rice to make 2 cups (500 ml) of cooked brown rice. Cooked rice freezes well, so be sure to stock up your freezer.

Nutrition Facts
Per serving

Amount	
Calories	607 kcal
Fat	19 g
Sodium	853 mg
Carbohydrate	62 g
Fiber	6 g
Protein	45 g

RICE NOODLES
with Smoked Oysters

1 serving • PREPARATION: 10 minutes • COOKING TIME: 10 minutes

INGREDIENTS

3 oz (90 g) rice noodles

1 can (3 oz/85 g) smoked oysters

½ tsp curry powder

1 tbsp sesame seeds

1 tbsp maple syrup

½ tsp sambal oelek

1 tsp lime juice

½ green onion, sliced

METHOD

In a large saucepan of boiling water over high heat, cook rice noodles for 3 to 5 minutes until al dente.

Meanwhile, drain oysters and reserve oil.

In a nonstick skillet over high heat, heat reserved oyster oil, curry powder and sesame seeds for 1 minute. Add maple syrup and sambal oelek. Continue cooking until large bubbles begin to appear on surface of maple syrup. Add oysters and sauté for 30 seconds or until lightly coated with sauce. Remove from heat, then sprinkle lime juice over mixture.

Serve oysters on rice noodles and garnish with sliced green onion.

• • • • • • • • • • • • •

TIP

Using smoked oysters is a practical, eco-friendly and economical choice.

Nutrition Facts
Per serving

Amount	
Calories	610 kcal
Fat	20 g
Sodium	512 mg
Carbohydrate	97 g
Fiber	3 g
Protein	17 g

Banh Mi

2 servings • PREPARATION: 15 minutes • MARINADE: 30 minutes • FREEZING TIME: 2 hours
THAWING TIME: 2 hours

INGREDIENTS

2 submarine rolls

4 tsp mayonnaise

1 tsp Sriracha sauce

Several leaves fresh cilantro

1 green onion, sliced

For the marinated tofu

7 oz (210 g) firm tofu, cut in ½-inch (1 cm) slices

2 tbsp low-sodium soy sauce

1 tsp sesame oil

1 tsp chopped fresh ginger

For the marinated vegetables

2 tsp rice vinegar

2 tsp granulated sugar

1 carrot, julienned

1 seedless cucumber, sliced

METHOD

Freeze tofu in an airtight bag for 2 hours, then thaw in refrigerator for at least 2 hours (tofu becomes slightly yellow when frozen but returns to normal color after thawing).

On a clean cloth, gently press tofu slices to remove excess water. Place soy sauce, sesame oil and ginger in the airtight bag. Add tofu and let marinate for at least 30 minutes (the longer you marinate, the more flavorful the tofu).

Meanwhile, in a bowl, combine rice vinegar and sugar. Add carrot and cucumber. Let marinate for at least 30 minutes.

Spread mayonnaise and Sriracha sauce on rolls. Add marinated tofu, carrot and cucumber slices. Top with cilantro and green onion.

• • • • • • • • • • • • •

TIP

Freezing then thaning the tofu helps it absorb the marinade better.

Nutrition Facts	
Per serving	
Amount	
Calories	344 kcal
Fat	19 g
Sodium	709 mg
Carbohydrate	35 g
Fiber	6 g
Protein	24 g

Blade Steak

6 servings • PREPARATION: 30 minutes • COOKING TIME: 4 hours

METHOD

Position rack in middle of oven and preheat to 350°F (180°C).

Heat oil in a Dutch oven on stovetop over medium-high heat. Season both sides of blade steak with salt and pepper. Place in Dutch oven. Add star anise and fennel seeds. Brown blade steak for 3 to 4 minutes on each side. Remove blade steak and spices from Dutch oven. Set aside.

In Dutch oven over medium heat, sauté onion and squash for 5 minutes or until onion becomes translucent. Add tomatoes and soy sauce. Stir, then place blade steak over vegetables. Cover and bring to a boil.

Cover and cook in middle of preheated oven for 4 hours. About 45 minutes before end of cooking time, add potatoes. Stir and continue cooking, uncovered, until meat shreds easily.

• • • • • • • • • • • • •

TIP

Use leftovers to prepare sandwiches (see Shredded Beef Sandwiches with Napa Cabbage Salad, p. 182).

INGREDIENTS

1 tbsp canola oil
2 lb (1 kg) flat iron (boneless beef top blade) steak
Salt and pepper
4 star anise pods
1 tsp fennel seeds
1 onion, diced
3½ cups (830 ml) diced butternut squash
1 can (28 oz/796 ml) diced tomatoes
1 tbsp low-sodium soy sauce
3 large potatoes, peeled and quartered

Nutrition Facts
Per serving

Amount	
Calories	546 kcal
Fat	21 g
Sodium	395 mg
Carbohydrate	53 g
Fiber	6 g
Protein	39 g

SALMON CUBES
and Quinoa

4 servings • PREPARATION: 20 minutes • MARINADE: 2 hours • COOKING TIME: 30 minutes

INGREDIENTS

¼ cup (60 ml) low-sodium soy sauce

2 tbsp canola oil

1 tsp sesame oil

1 tbsp lemon juice

2 tbsp chopped fresh ginger

1⅓ lbs (600 g) fresh salmon fillet, skin removed and cut into 1-inch (2.5 cm) cubes

For the Quinoa

1 tsp canola oil

1 yellow onion, diced

1 cup (250 ml) quinoa

1⅓ cups (325 ml) chicken broth

1 tbsp chopped fresh cilantro

Pinch salt

¼ tsp black pepper

METHOD

In a large airtight bag, combine soy sauce, canola oil, sesame oil, lemon juice and ginger. Add salmon cubes and let marinate in the refrigerator for about 2 hours (avoid marinating for longer than 2 hours or the salmon will taste too salty).

Position rack in middle of oven and pre-heat broiler. Line a baking sheet with parchment paper.

Meanwhile, heat canola oil in a sauce-pan over medium-high heat and brown onion. Add quinoa and stir for 1 minute until lightly toasted. Add chicken broth and bring to a boil. Cover and cook over low heat for 18 minutes. Remove from heat and fluff quinoa with a fork. Let rest for 5 minutes. Add cilantro, then season with salt and pepper.

Drain salmon cubes and place on prepared baking sheet. Cook in middle of oven for 10 minutes.

Serve salmon with quinoa.

Nutrition Facts	
Per serving	
Amount	
Calories	545 kcal
Fat	28 g
Sodium	573 mg
Carbohydrate	34 g
Fiber	4 g
Protein	38 g

GEMELLI
Carbonara

2 servings • PREPARATION: 10 minutes • COOKING TIME: 15 minutes

INGREDIENTS

1¾ cups (425 ml) gemelli

⅓ cup (80 ml) ham, cut into strips

1 clove garlic, chopped

3 eggs, lightly beaten

Black pepper

½ cup (125 ml) grated Parmesan cheese

METHOD

In a large saucepan, cook pasta according to package directions or until al dente. Drain.

In same saucepan over medium heat, sauté ham and garlic for 2 to 3 minutes.

Remove from heat. Add pasta and stir. Add eggs and season with pepper. Stir and sprinkle with Parmesan cheese.

Nutrition Facts Per serving	
Amount	
Calories	583 kcal
Fat	19 g
Sodium	871 mg
Carbohydrate	67 g
Fiber	3 g
Protein	35 g

SHREDDED BEEF SANDWICHES
with Napa Cabbage Salad

2 servings • PREPARATION: 15 minutes • COOKING TIME: 5 minutes

INGREDIENTS

5 oz (150 g) Star Anise Blade Steak, cooked and shredded (see p. 177)

2 pita breads

1 large dill pickle, sliced

1 oz (30 g) Brie cheese

For the Cabbage Salad

2 tbsp vinegar

2 tbsp canola oil

2 tbsp granulated sugar

1 tsp dry mustard

Pinch salt

¼ tsp black pepper

4 cups (1 l) thinly sliced napa cabbage (Chinese cabbage)

1 carrot, grated

1 tbsp chopped onion

2 tsp sesame seeds

METHOD

In a small saucepan over high heat, bring vinegar, oil, sugar, mustard, salt and pepper to a boil.

Meanwhile, in a bowl, combine cabbage, carrot and onion.

Pour warm vinaigrette over vegetables. Sprinkle with sesame seeds. Refrigerate.

Reheat beef in microwave for 45 to 60 seconds or until beef is warm.

Fill pitas with shredded beef, pickles and cheese. Serve with cabbage salad.

Nutrition Facts
Per serving

Amount	
Calories	522 kcal
Fat	19 g
Sodium	755 mg
Carbohydrate	50 g
Fiber	5 g
Protein	37 g

PESTO
Couscous

1 serving • PREPARATION: 10 minutes • COOKING TIME: 5 minutes

INGREDIENTS

1 tsp canola oil

3 oz (90 g) boneless skinless chicken breast, cut into strips

⅓ cup (80 ml) uncooked couscous

⅓ cup (80 ml) chicken broth

⅓ cup (80 ml) water

1 cup (250 ml) frozen vegetables

2 tbsp tomato paste

2 tsp basil pesto

Salt and pepper

METHOD

Heat oil in a skillet over high heat. Add chicken, season to taste and cook for 3 minutes. Turn over chicken strips and continue cooking for 2 minutes.

Meanwhile, in a large microwave-safe cup, combine couscous, chicken broth, water, vegetables, tomato paste and pesto. Cook in microwave for 3 minutes on High (1200 watts).

Mix together chicken and couscous.

• • • • • • • • • • • • •

TIP

Frozen vegetables are convenient, nutritious and easy to use. You can choose from several varieties of diced mixed vegetables.

Nutrition Facts
Per serving

Amount	
Calories	532 kcal
Fat	10 g
Sodium	661 mg
Carbohydrate	76 g
Fiber	11 g
Protein	37 g

SHRIMP AND SQUASH
Risotto

4 servings • PREPARATION: 20 minutes • COOKING TIME: 1 hour

METHOD

Position rack in middle of oven and preheat to 350°F (180°C). Line a baking sheet with parchment paper.

Place squash, cut side down, on prepared baking sheet. Cook in middle of oven for 40 minutes. Allow to cool before removing flesh, then set aside.

Meanwhile, heat oil in a saucepan over medium-high heat and sauté onion for 4 minutes. Add rice and stir for 1 minute.

Reduce heat to medium. Add 1 cup (250 ml) of the chicken broth to saucepan and stir. Cover and let simmer for 3 to 4 minutes. Add another cup (250 ml) of chicken broth and stir. Cover and let simmer for 3 to 4 minutes. Continue until all broth has been added.

Remove from heat. Add diced squash and Parmesan cheese. Mix, then add shrimp. Let heat for 5 minutes. Season with pepper.

INGREDIENTS

½ acorn squash, seeds removed

¼ cup (60 ml) olive oil

1 onion, chopped

1 cup (250 ml) risotto rice

4 cups (1 l) chicken broth, hot, divided

½ cup (125 ml) grated Parmesan cheese

1 lb (500 g) frozen Nordic shrimp

Black pepper

Nutrition Facts	
Per serving	
Amount	
Calories	414 kcal
Fat	6 g
Sodium	743 mg
Carbohydrate	54 g
Fiber	3 g
Protein	34 g

CURRIED TOFU SALAD
Sandwiches

2 servings • PREPARATION: 10 minutes

INGREDIENTS

4 slices whole-grain bread

2 slices Emmental cheese

2 leaves iceberg lettuce

For the Tofu Salad

8 oz (250 g) firm tofu

⅓ cup (80 ml) Greek yogurt, plain

1 carrot, grated

1 green onion, sliced

2 tsp maple syrup

1 tsp curry powder

Pinch salt

METHOD

In a food processor, combine all tofu salad ingredients and purée.

To assemble sandwiches, divide tofu salad evenly on two slices of bread. Top each with a slice of cheese and lettuce leaf. Cover with another slice of bread.

SPORTS INFO

•••

Two or three days prior to a major sporting event, you should decrease your consumption of whole-grain products in order to prevent any gastrointestinal discomfort. Whole-grain bread can be replaced with white bread.

Nutrition Facts	
Per serving	
Amount	
Calories	416 kcal
Fat	14 g
Sodium	496 mg
Carbohydrate	44 g
Fiber	6 g
Protein	31 g

SALMON AND DILL
Spaghetti

3 servings • PREPARATION: 10 minutes • COOKING TIME: 15 minutes

INGREDIENTS

8 oz (250 g) spaghetti

1 tbsp olive oil

1 yellow onion, diced

1 clove garlic, chopped

1 can (7½ oz/213 g) salmon, drained

1 tbsp paprika

1 tbsp capers

½ cup (125 ml) table (18%) cream

2 tbsp lemon juice

4 tbsp chopped fresh dill

METHOD

Cook pasta in a large saucepan of boiling water over high heat for 8 minutes or until al dente. Drain and set aside.

Meanwhile, heat oil in a large nonstick skillet over medium-high heat and brown onion. Add garlic and sauté for 1 minute. Add salmon and paprika and sauté for 1 minute. Reduce heat to medium-low and add capers, cream and lemon juice. Let simmer for 5 minutes. Add dill and stir.

Add spaghetti and coat well with sauce.

• • • • • • • • • • • • •

TIP

There is no need to remove any fine bones you may find in the fish as they can be easily crushed with a fork.

SPORTS INFO

The day before a sporting event, and up to three days prior, it is important to eat carb-rich foods such as potatoes, pastas and grain products (rice, couscous, barley, cereal, bread, etc.)

Nutrition Facts Per serving	
Amount	
Calories	534 kcal
Fat	16 g
Sodium	378 mg
Carbohydrate	70 g
Fiber	3 g
Protein	28 g

ABOUT
the Authors

Philippe Grand and Stéphanie Côté are both registered dietitians at Extenso, the nutrition research center at Université de Montréal. Because they work together, they know each other well and can leverage each other's strengths. For example, Philippe is a better cook than Stéphanie because he graduated from the Institut du Tourisme et d'Hôtellerie du Québec (ITHQ). After training as a chef, he worked in the restaurant business for several years. So he knows more – quite a bit more – than Stéphanie when it comes to the kitchen, which is why he developed most of the recipes in this book. Though he is a connoisseur with a refined palate, he did agree to a few very good recipes submitted by his friend and colleague.

Stéphanie writes better than Philippe. In 2000, she was awarded the Fernand-Seguin Fellowship, which recognizes emerging talents in scientific reporting. She worked for Protégez-Vous, Ricardo, Naître et grandir and other media outlets where she put her skills to good use. Stéphanie also has a master's degree in sports nutrition, so she handled the part of the book that addresses theory. She graciously accepted some of Philippe's comments.

When it comes to sports, Stéphanie runs faster and further than Philippe, but he has more physical strength. On cross-country skis, they move at the same speed, although Philippe is slightly less aerodynamic because of the icicles that form in his beard.

stephaniecote.ca
extenso.org

ACKNOWLEDGMENTS

When food and sports are among your greatest passions, you feel privileged to write a book about sports nutrition. So we are very grateful to Groupe Modus, and especially Isabelle Jodoin and Marc G. Alain, for entrusting us with this project. Thank you to Nolwenn Gouezel for copy-editing the manuscript and for ensuring that not a single comma is missing from the recipes or the copy. And for this English version, we want to thank Brandie Brunner, Kristin Cairns and Carol Sherman.

Thank you to food stylist Gabrielle Dalessandro and to photographer André Noël. Photos make all the difference in a cookbook. And because we wanted to look as good as the food, our thanks go to Katy St-Laurent for the KSL apparel and to David Moore for our portrait.

A very special thanks to our friends and colleagues Évelyne Deblock and Martin Fréchette for making sure our information was correct. You will find the contact information for both of them on the next page.

RESOURCES
for Athletes

SPORTS NUTRITIONISTS
Évelyne Deblock, RD, M.Sc.
www.equilibre2.com
info@equilibre2.com

Martin Fréchette, RD, M.Sc.
mfrechette.nutrition@gmail.com

Nutrium Clinique Universitaire de Nutrition
www.cliniquenutrition.umontreal.ca

OTHER WEBSITES
Coaching Association of Canada
www.coach.ca

Gatorade Sports Science Institute
www.gssiweb.org/en

Dietitians of Canada
www.dietitians.ca

My Sport Science, Asker Jeukendrup, sports nutritionist
www.mysportscience.com

Sports Dietitians Australia
www.sportsdietitians.com.au

Australian Sports Commission
www.ausport.gov.au/ais/nutrition

The Association of UK Dietitians
www.sportsdietitians.org.uk

SUGGESTED READING

Nancy Clark, *Nancy Clark's Sports Nutrition Guidebook* (5th Edition), Human Kinetics, 2013.

Suzanne Girard Eberle, *Endurance Sports Nutrition* (3rd Edition), Human Kinetics, 2014.

Marielle Ledoux, Geneviève St-Martin and Natalie Lacombe, *Nutrition sport et performance,* Collection Géo Plein Air, 2009.

RECIPE Index

KNOW WHAT TO EAT

A diet suited to your needs based on advice from expert dietitians

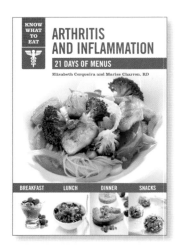